The Shyness Workbook for Teens

Bernardo J. Carducci • Teesue H. Fields

Research Press • 2612 North Mattis Avenue • Champaign, Illinois 61822
(800) 519-2707 • www.researchpress.com

Copies of this book may be ordered from Research Press at the address given on the title page.

Composition by Jeff Helgesen
Cover design by Linda Brown, Positive I.D. Graphic Design, Inc.
Printed by Malloy, Inc.

ISBN-13: 978–0–87822–583–5
ISBN-10: 0–87822–583–8

*For Rozana, a daughter whose love inspires me
to be a better educator, mentor, and friend to the shy
and non-shy alike.*

—BJC

*This book is dedicated to my husband,
Glenn, and my sons, Michael and Aaron.*

—THF

Contents

Preface

Words of Welcome and a Plan of Action

From Bernie Carducci:

As a shy teenager, I began reading about shyness in college in an attempt to do something about it for myself. My initial interest in shyness for purely personal reasons has turned into a professional pursuit for the past 25 years. In my pursuit to understand the nature and dynamics of shyness, one of the most fascinating aspects of shyness I found is its pervasiveness. More specifically, my research over the years in the study of shyness, along with the research of others, indicates that approximately 40 percent of the general population describes itself as shy, and about 95 percent of the overall population reports to know firsthand what it means to be shy in some situations or at some point in their lives. So chances are pretty good that either you are shy or you know individuals who are or have been shy.

Another critical aspect of shyness is the pain and difficulty it can cause you and other shy individuals in those areas of their lives that are central to a sense of happiness, such as establishing friendships and intimate relationships, pursuing educational and career opportunities, and fostering personal and family relationships over a lifetime. Through talking with teens and adults, I have become convinced that adolescence is a crucial time for learning to deal with shyness. So many adults identify adolescence as the time when they felt defeated by their shyness and developed habits that followed them as adults. As one college senior told me after a workshop, "If I could have just learned some of these skills early in high school, maybe I wouldn't still think of those years as the worst of my life."

Although shy individuals are perceived as passive and withdrawn, my research indicates that many shy teens try to take action to deal with their shyness. However, a characteristic feature of much of the action they take is that it is based on an incomplete understanding of what shyness is and how it works and, as a result, how it tends to work against the best interests of these shy teens. Performing such ineffective actions can produce less than satisfying results, which leads to a sense of frustration and hopelessness. Again, I have no doubt that you have probably tried many solutions to deal with your shyness that have left you feeling less than satisfied and a little more than frustrated, which is probably why you decided to utilize *The Shyness Workbook for Teens.*

Much of the information presented in *The Shyness Workbook for Teens* is based on my other books on the subject of shyness, including *Shyness: A Bold New Approach* (HarperCollins, 2000); *The Shyness Breakthrough* (Rodale, 2003); *The Shyness Workbook: 30 Days to Dealing Effectively with Shyness* (Research Press, 2005); and *The Pocket Guide to Making Successful Small Talk: How to Talk to Anyone Anytime Anywhere About Anything* (Pocket Guide Publishing, 1999b). Even though *The Shyness Workbook for Teens* is designed to help you and other shy teens understand and respond more successfully to your shyness, you may find it helpful to expand your knowledge of shyness gained through *The Shyness Workbook for Teens* by reading any of these other books cited here.

From Teesue Fields:

Before coming to the university to teach, I worked as a psychologist, trying to help children and adolescents feel more comfortable in their worlds. I was always drawn to those whose shyness made it hard for them to overcome other problems. I think this is because I was shy, particularly from middle school through college. I was comfortable in small groups, or when I knew people really well, or when I had a clear role to play (like ushering at a play). I could talk to people individually, but felt very uncomfortable at parties or dances, especially when I didn't know many people. My best strategy was to pick somebody who looked even more shy and uncomfortable than I did and then talk to him or her. I did not get a better understanding of myself until I was in graduate school in psychology and was trying to learn how to help other people. Although I feel I am now more "successfully shy," I still have to be aware of my shyness and find strategies to deal with it, especially in new situations.

As a university teacher, I encounter shy students in every class, and I can see the problems their shyness causes them, even though they might have good academic skills. As the mother of two sons, I am also aware of how hard it is for one to help teens deal with their shyness, even when one is around those teens every day. When counseling teens, it is obvious that shyness has a very negative effect on how comfortable teens feel in school. We know that students who do not have friends and do not participate in school activities are much more likely to drop out of school. And one of the reasons that teens fail to make friends or participate in school activities is their shyness.

✳ ✣ ✳

From Bernie and Teesue:

The Shyness Workbook for Teens can be used by you and other shy teens to learn more about shyness and to discover ways to deal with shyness. It can also be used by school counselors, psychologists, and therapists who are working with shy teens. The information and activities in this workbook have been designed to speak specifically to shy teens in an effort to help them become "successfully shy."

Successfully shy teens learn to control their shyness instead of letting their shyness control them. To help you and other shy teens become successfully shy, *The Shyness Workbook for Teens* contains a series of 30 separate daily units designed to provide the type of information that will make it possible for you to respond more effectively to your shyness. Each daily unit contains four elements. The first is titled "What You Need to Know" and includes some core information about a particular area of shyness. The next element—"Your Turn"—contains a variety of self-directed activities and self-scoring quizzes and inventories to help you examine your own shyness. The third element is a feature titled "Voices." The "voices" are composites of interviews and surveys with shy teens intended to help you see that you are not alone in your struggle with shyness. Finally, these three elements lead into a "Journal" activity that asks you to think about what you have learned and apply it to your own life.

The workbook is divided into three parts. "Part I: Meet Your Shy Self" is an introduction to shyness that will help you explore and examine the nature of your own shyness. "Part II: What's Going On? The Underlying Dynamics of Shyness" is designed to provide you with a basic understanding of shyness. "Part III: Strategies for Successfully Shy Teens" presents a number of different strategies that will help you to control your shyness instead of letting your shyness control you. The epilogue, "Living the Successfully Shy Life," is a wrap-up that includes a plan for developing your next steps that go beyond this workbook and into your life as a "successfully shy teen." It is important to start at the beginning so that you have a clear understanding of what your particular shyness is like and how it affects you because shyness is different for each person. By the time you have worked through all the units, you should have in mind a clear plan for becoming "successfully shy."

As you begin your journey, please do not be shy about contacting us. We welcome your comments and look forward to hearing from you regarding your progress. We can be reached by e-mail at <u>shydoc@carducci.com</u> or by sending a letter to us at the following address:

The Shyness Enrichment Institute
PO Box 8064
New Albany, IN 47151-8064

Again, we look forward to hearing from you.

Bernie Carducci and Teesue Fields

Acknowledgments

Some Expressions of Gratitude

From Bernardo Carducci:

The Shyness Workbook for Teens is the product of the collective efforts of many different individuals. First and foremost, I want to acknowledge my coauthor, Teesue Fields.

As a longtime colleague, I was aware of the dedication that Teesue always brings to anything that she is involved with at the university and in the community. So working on this project for me was made more easy and enjoyable because of her involvement. While this is our first collaborative effort, I hope it will not be our last.

I am also fortunate to work with a group of exceptional reference librarians at the university who know how to find the information I need in a truly expeditious manner. I am grateful to Marty Rosen, Gabrielle Carr, Jacqueline Johnson, Melanie Hughes, Bonita Mason, Jim Jenkins, and especially Nancy Totten for their continued professional support and personal friendship.

Once again, I acknowledge the "Lunch Bunch"—Lesley Deal, Kathleen Norvell, and Brigette Colligan—for making lunch more about laughs than about food.

Rozana Carducci, my daughter, confidante, and soon-to-be colleague, keeps me excited about my academic activities as she shares with me the excitement she has for her academic activities. I am grateful to Seth Taper for worrying about my daughter so that I do not have to worry as much.

* ❋ *

From Teesue Fields:

I am fortunate that I work in a very nurturing environment. I teach in a graduate program in counseling where the students are working adults who bring their own skills and knowledge to the courses. They challenge, encourage, and tolerate me. I also work on a campus that values teaching and makes collaboration possible between disciplines. This book is just such a collaboration. Bernie Carducci has been incredibly generous in sharing his years of research and vast fund of knowledge about shyness with me. And he has been very open to making this book as easy to read as possible for adolescents. We quickly established a comfortable partnership of writing together that made working on this book a pleasure.

I am also fortunate that I had parents who loved me and encouraged me to stretch myself both intellectually and emotionally. I was a shy bookworm, but I still felt valued. I gradually became more comfortable with other people, at least in some situations, and I learned to accept that at times I wouldn't be comfortable. It was a good thing I was drawn to studying psychology and counseling because I learned a lot about myself while I tried to learn how to help others.

But the place I have learned the most about myself is in my own family as a wife and as a mother to two sons. Here again, I have been very fortunate because I am surrounded every day by love, concern, and laughter, both in person and when distance separates us through e-mail and cell phones. It takes a lot of help and just the right environment to produce a book; I had all I could have wished for.

From Bernardo and Teesue:

Finally, there are a few folks at Research Press who deserve to be recognized. We thank David Hamburg for his skillful editorial advice. Jeff Helgesen handled the production details in a seamless manner that made it possible for many different individuals and departments to work together in harmony, even when under strict deadlines. We thank Dennis Wiziecki for the exceptional job he does of "getting the word out" about our work. Finally, Russell Pence is always so supportive and encouraging, especially when he says, "OK, now that this is done, what are we going to do next?" Those are the words that authors dream of hearing from a publisher.

To all of our family members, friends, and colleagues, we say thanks for helping us to help shy teens help themselves to become successfully shy.

Part I

Meet Your Shy Self

DAY 1 What Is Shyness?

What You Need to Know

Before you can start your journey toward dealing with your shyness, you have to understand what shyness is and what it is not. The information presented below will help you learn the distinction:

Question: Are the following statements true or false?

> Shyness is a disease.
>
> Shyness is a character flaw.
>
> A shy person is the same as an introvert.

Answer: All of these statements are false.

What Is a Shy Person?

A shy person is someone who truly wants to be with others but finds it difficult to do so. For example, a shy person may have trouble talking to someone he or she is attracted to or wants to get to know. Because shyness keeps people from doing something they want to do, the shy person is unhappy about his or her shyness.

Is a Shy Person an Introvert?

An introvert is someone who likes being alone and is happy doing things alone. The introvert will spend a lot of time by himself or herself. A shy person wants to be around other people but feels uncomfortable and, as noted, has trouble doing so.

To help you make the distinction between shyness and introversion, consider this example: At a party, the shy person is standing alone but looks uncomfortable. ("I wish I had the nerve to talk to somebody. I wish somebody would come and talk to me.")

The introvert is standing alone but looks content. ("Don't bother me. I'm happy just standing here holding up this wall.") Actually, it is unlikely that the introvert would go to a party at all, but that's another story.

As this example illustrates, what shyness really comes down to is a matter of control. For shy individuals, their shyness controls them and prevents them from doing things such as making friends, having dates, getting a part-time job, or joining with others in school activities. What you must strive to learn—and what we want this workbook to help you to learn—is how to control your shyness instead of letting it control you. In other words, you must learn to be successfully shy.

How Shy Are You?

Some people feel shy most of the time, whereas others feel shy only in certain situations. Before you try to deal with your shyness, it helps to understand how much of a problem it is for you. To help you understand your shyness, take *The Shyness Quiz,* which follows.

Your Turn

The Shyness Quiz

Complete The Shyness Quiz *by simply circling the number that best represents your answer to each of the questions presented:*

How often do you feel shy?

1. Once a month or less
2. Every other day or so
3. All the time—several times a day

Compared to other kids you know, how shy are you?

1. Much less shy
2. About as shy
3. Much more shy

"When I feel shy, my heart races and my palms sweat."

1. This is not true for me.
2. This is sometimes true for me.
3. This is true most of the time for me.

"When I feel shy, I think people are rating negatively everything I say and do."

1. This is not true for me.
2. This is sometimes true for me.
3. This is true most of the time for me.

"Shyness keeps me from doing what I want to in social settings—like being able to talk to people."

1. This is not true for me.
2. This is sometimes true for me.
3. This is true most of the time for me.

"I feel shy when I am around someone I really like."

1. This is not true for me.
2. This is sometimes true for me.
3. This is true most of the time for me.

(Continued next page)

"I feel shy when I am around someone in a position of authority, like a teacher, a coach, or a boss."

1. This is not true for me.
2. This is sometimes true for me.
3. This is true most of the time for me.

Your Shyness Score: _____

To determine your shyness score for the quiz, take a piece of scratch paper and simply add all of your circled responses together. Now, compare your score with those below to see what your shyness score tells you about your shyness.

If your score is 7–12: Your shyness is normal. Most of the time you are not shy.

If your score is 13–18: You experience a lot of shyness in your life. This workbook will help you when you encounter difficult situations.

If your score is 19–21: You are a very shy person. By using this workbook and putting in a lot of effort, you can overcome your shyness.

Voices

"I went to the first meeting of the Drama Club last week. When I came in the room, everyone was talking to somebody else. I didn't know anybody, so I just sat down in the back of the room. Not a single person talked to me the entire time. I don't know if I want to go back."

—Betty, a high school student

"I'd love to be able to go to the high school football games, but my two friends don't like football. All the students sit together in one big section, and I know some middle school students go because I hear them talking about it. I guess I could go and try to find some people I know, but what if nobody wants me to sit with them and they just ignore me? I'd feel horrible."

—Jeff, an eighth-grade student

Journal

Think about the most recent time that you felt really shy and your shyness prevented you from doing something you wanted to do. Now answer these questions in the space provided:

What was the event?

_____

_____

_____

Who else was there?

_____

_____

_____

What did you want to be able to do?

_____

_____

_____

What were you afraid would happen if you did it?

_____

_____

_____

DAY 2   Are You Born Shy?

What You Need to Know

Have you ever seen a shy baby? Probably not. Remember all those smiling baby pictures parents and friends have shown you? How about a shy three-year-old? Sure. For example, you might meet a three-year-old at church, and he grabs his parent's legs and hides his face. What about a shy 10-year-old? Again, yes. He or she might be the kid who stands on the sidelines at recess and doesn't get to play any games. How about a shy 14-year-old? Of course. That would be the teenager who goes to the party but won't ask anybody to dance. As you grow up, your shyness remains the same, but the situations that trigger your shyness change.

A common question shy teens have about shyness is "Are you born shy?" No! You are not born shy. You develop feelings of shyness as you grow up. There are a variety of situations that can make people feel shy. Sometimes they happen within the family; other times they occur at school.

One familiar situation involves the kind of treatment you receive from your peers. In school, for example, if other people laugh at you when you answer a teacher's question incorrectly, that can trigger your shyness. As a result, you may be afraid to talk in class in the future. Another common situation at school is your being uncertain what to say when you want to meet a new student or introduce yourself to a student you've always wanted to get to know.

At home, meanwhile, if your family is the kind that doesn't socialize much, you will become accustomed to being around very few people. Therefore, your shyness is triggered again. As the examples in this workbook will illustrate, there are lots of situations that trigger shyness, but being born shy is not one of them.

If you're not born shy, then why are you shy? You're shy because, like other shy people, you think that most everyone is looking at you and thinking or saying bad things about you. Soon you come to believe that others are always judging what you are doing. In truth, all of these situations have as their basis a sense of self. A sense of self (who I am and how I'm different from the other people in my world) does not develop in infants until they are at least 18 months of age. So because you are not born with a sense of self, you cannot be born shy.

Your Turn

Instead of believing that you are born shy, try taking a closer look at certain situations that have served as "shyness triggers" and that might have contributed to your shyness. Think about the following and write down your thoughts in the space provided:

1. Describe a time when you felt very self-conscious (for example, when you had to give a talk in class, or when you had to meet your new stepfather's relatives):

2. Describe a couple of situations in which you felt some negative things about yourself (for example, when you went to see a basketball game by yourself and thought that your clothes looked all wrong or your hair looked horrible).

   Situation:

   Negative thoughts:

   Situation:

   Negative thoughts:

3. Identify a couple of situations in which you felt that everyone was judging you, and then list what you think they were saying about you (for example, during your first day at a new school or shortly after you arrive at a party).

   Situation:

   Judgmental comments:

   Situation:

   Judgmental comments:

Voices

"I've always been uncomfortable about my red hair. It really makes me stand out in a crowd. My parents won't let me dye it. But I am sure that if I had regular brown hair, I wouldn't feel so shy because I could just blend in with others."

—Emily, a sixth-grade student

"I have a really big family, and we get together for holidays and birthdays at my grandma and grandpa's house. It's basically the same 40 people every time, but the adults always have lots of questions about what I'm doing, and the older kids are always teasing me about something. My sister loves going and seems to have such a good time. But I always feel uncomfortable."

—Rory, a ninth-grade student

Journal

Think of the very first time that you remember feeling shy and then answer these questions:

1. How old were you? _____

_____

2. What was the occasion? _____

_____

3. Who was there? _____

_____

4. What did your shy feelings make you want to do? _____

_____

_____

5. What did you end up doing? _____

_____

6. Did others say or do something to make you feel even more uncomfortable? What did they say?

_____

_____

7. Did certain people help you feel more comfortable? What did they do?

_____

_____

DAY 3 Is Shyness All in Your Head?

What You Need to Know

Consider the following chat between Bettina and Rafael:

Bettina: I just feel so shy when I'm meeting new people. I wish I were more comfortable.

Rafael: Just tell yourself that it will be fine. If you believe positive things will happen, then you won't feel shy.

But Rafael is wrong. Shyness is not just in your head. Shyness includes reactions of your body, such as a racing heart and dry mouth and butterflies in your stomach. Shyness also includes feelings about yourself, such as how well you feel you are performing in social situations and how you think others are reacting to you. In addition, shyness includes thoughts about your behavior, such as your ability to approach other people and your ability to start and sustain conversations.

In short, shyness includes shyness of your body, shyness of your thoughts, and shyness of your behavior. Therefore, if you deal with only one part of shyness, such as your thoughts (for example, "Believe positive things will happen"), then you won't really be able to deal with your shyness effectively. Here are some examples of typical "quick fixes" for shyness:

+ Think happy thoughts.
+ Take deep breaths.
+ Go someplace where there are people; someone is sure to talk to you.
+ Just force yourself to go up to someone and say hello.

Sometimes these quick fixes will work, but more often than not, they won't. In fact, using some of these quick fixes might make you feel even more shy. Why? When these quick fixes do not work, you feel even more shy because you tried and failed—your shyness is still controlling you. For example, it is not enough to go to the party and tell yourself you are bound to meet someone. Instead, you need to know how to approach someone and then how to start and maintain a conversation.

In this workbook, we are going to deal effectively with shyness, not by offering quick fixes that often fail, but by helping you understand your shyness and providing strategies that deal with the three types of shyness: (a) shyness of the body, (b) shyness of the mind, and (c) shyness of behavior.

Your Turn

Go back and look at that recent incident you described in your journal during Day 1. Read through it again. Now answer the following questions, each of which is related to one of the types of shyness discussed.

Shyness of the Body: What kinds of sensations did you have in your body when you felt shy in this situation (for example, dry mouth, sweaty palms, racing heart, shaky hands, wobbly knees)?

_____

_____

Shyness of the Mind: What thoughts were running through your mind in this situation (for example, "Everybody is looking at me" or "People can sense how really nervous I am")?

_____

_____

Shyness of Behavior: How did you generally evaluate your behavior in this kind of situation (for example, "I don't know what to say when I meet people" or "Sometimes I can talk for a sentence or two, and then I run out of things to say")?

_____

_____

Your Strategy: What, if anything, did you do to deal with your shyness in this situation, and how well did it work?

_____

_____

Voices

"I started to talk during the class discussion the other day. I always think that nobody will want to hear what I have to say, but this time I kept telling myself, 'It's OK, this is something good. They'll like this.' But when I tried to raise my hand, my arm was so wobbly and my throat was so dry that I pulled it down quick before anybody could see it. I felt like such a dork."

—Inez, a high school sophomore

"When I walk into a party, I feel like everybody is looking at me. Suddenly I start getting worried about what I'm wearing and how my hair looks. I mean, I have a really lousy sense of style. I know I don't dress right. And sometimes I just feel stuck right there at the door. I mean my legs just don't even want to move."

—Nancy, a high school senior

"I like biology class because we work in small groups and talk about the lab assignment we have. I don't have to think about what to say because we are just trying to do the assignment. But once we finish and people start talking about other stuff, I don't know what to talk about. Why would anybody want to hear about my boring life?"

—Matt, a ninth-grade student

Journal

List some of the "quick fixes" people have suggested to you or that you have tried to use to deal with your shyness. After each one, describe which shyness—shyness of the body, shyness of the mind, or shyness of behavior—and which aspect of that shyness was addressed by it.

Quick fix No. 1: _____

Type of shyness and aspect of that shyness:

_____

_____

_____

Quick fix No. 2: _____

Type of shyness and aspect of that shyness:

_____

_____

_____

Quick fix No. 3: _____

Type of shyness and aspect of that shyness:

_____

_____

_____

Part II

What's Going On?
The Underlying Dynamics of Shyness

DAY 4   Why Does Shyness Hurt?

What You Need to Know

Shyness hurts because it involves a kind of self-defeating contest between pushing and pulling, which is called an "approach-avoidance conflict." This conflict means that when shy people feel a strong desire to do something with other people, such as talk to strangers at a party or approach somebody they are attracted to, they simultaneously feel an equally strong desire to avoid the situation because it might end in rejection or ridicule.

Your heart tells you, "It would be fun to go to that party and talk to people," while at the same time, your head says, "Don't you dare. Nobody would talk to you. People will probably laugh at you." You want to be around others, but you are afraid you won't be comfortable or won't know what to say. You decide that no matter how much you want to do *something,* the safest thing to do is *nothing.* That's because in your mind you are thinking that the less you do or say, the fewer reasons people will have to reject you.

On the other hand, the more you want to be with others and the more your shyness holds you back, the more hurt you feel. This is your approach-avoidance conflict. One way to evaluate your desire to get past this conflict is to see how willing you are to take social risks.

Your Turn

Assessing Your Tolerance for Risk

On a scale of 1 (totally unlike me) to 5 (totally like me), rate yourself on the following:

1. It's easy for me to approach total strangers and start talking to them.

   Unlike me   1   2   3   4   5   Like me

2. I enjoy being the center of attention.

   Unlike me   1   2   3   4   5   Like me

3. If I disagree with someone, I will let him or her know.

   Unlike me   1   2   3   4   5   Like me

4. I don't mind being one of the first people on the dance floor.

   Unlike me   1   2   3   4   5   Like me

5. I usually don't worry about being put down for what I do or say in public.

   Unlike me   1   2   3   4   5   Like me

6. If I'm attracted to someone, I let him or her know about it.

   Unlike me   1   2   3   4   5   Like me

7. I don't mind going to a party or a dance or a sports event alone.

   Unlike me   1   2   3   4   5   Like me

8. I look forward to meeting new people wherever I go.

   Unlike me   1   2   3   4   5   Like me

9. I don't worry about doing something stupid at a party or a dance because most people won't remember.

   Unlike me   1   2   3   4   5   Like me

10. I usually don't hold my feelings back when I'm around people.

    Unlike me   1   2   3   4   5   Like me

The higher your score (35–50), the more likely you are to take risks with other people. If your score was on the low end (10–25), you're probably avoiding new encounters because you believe they're too unpredictable and dangerous. The key is to take a risk when you are able to plan how to deal with that particular challenge. If you scored in the middle (26–34), there probably are some situations where you take risks and some where you don't. Regardless of your score, you can use this knowledge to help you when you're trying to figure out when to try to take risks in new social situations.

Voices

"I kept telling myself to go over and sit with those kids at lunch. There were only three of them and they seemed nice. They talk to me in class. But what if they tell me I can't sit with them? Or maybe I'd sit down and they wouldn't talk to me. It would feel awful. It's better just to sit by myself and read my book during lunch."

—Trina, a 12-year-old student

I'm really a pretty good dancer, but that's when I'm home in my own room. There are lots of kids out there just doing their own thing. Not really dancing with anybody, just working with the beat. I can do that. It feels so good to move with the lights and the music. But what if I get out there and people laugh at me? What if people move away from me and don't even want to be on the floor with me? I could never ever come here again. And I like coming here. So I just stay on the sidelines, watching other people dance."

—Jamal, a 16-year-old student

Journal

Describe a situation in the past year when your heart told you to take a social risk that was really important to you (for example, go to a party, audition for the chorus of the play), but your head told you not to, so you didn't take the risk.

What was your head telling you that stopped you from taking the risk?

Looking back at it now, what do you *really* think would have happened if you had taken that risk?

DAY 5   Taking Your Time

What You Need to Know

Think about the following situation:

Yolanda and her less shy friend stay after school to help set up for the science fair. Yolanda loves science, and her friend is with her, so she's been telling herself it should be OK. But when she gets to the gym, there are a lot more people than she expected, and she doesn't recognize most of them. And her science teacher isn't even there. Yolanda really wants to help, but this isn't a situation she was prepared for. Then Yolanda notices her friend has already gone over to a group of people and is talking to them. Yolanda just wants to turn around and leave.

So what's going on here? Although everybody needs some time to warm up and adjust to new situations, it seems that shy individuals need more time than individuals who are not shy in order to make that adjustment. This is especially true when a shy person feels that push and pull of the approach-avoidance conflict.

Yolanda is probably having unrealistic expectations for herself. Shy people seem to think they will magically turn into less shy people as soon as they enter a social situation. When they don't, they assume it's because they aren't good in social situations, so they quickly leave.

What should Yolanda do instead? She needs to recognize that it will take her a little longer than her friend to feel comfortable in this new situation. She could walk over and stand next to her friend, even if she isn't comfortable saying anything. She could walk around the room some by herself until she feels more comfortable. She could even stand right where she is and look for some other people she knows.

The next time she could even arrive a little early. That would give her some time to meet individuals one-on-one before everybody starts to split up into groups.

The important thing is that Yolanda give herself some time. She should also take care not to put herself down by comparing herself to her friend, who is less shy. There is nothing wrong with Yolanda; she just needs a little more time to adjust than most. And she's probably figured this out to some extent: When a shy teen recognizes what is happening and is patient with herself, then the teen has taken a big step toward learning to deal with shyness.

Your Turn

Describe some situations where you need to give yourself some time to warm up and adjust. List at least one thing you could do while you are adjusting to that situation.
Here's an example:

Situation: Somebody new walks up to my usual group of friends.
Warm-up strategy: Keep quiet and listen while my friends talk. When I feel comfortable, I will ask a friendly question, such as "Where did you get those sunglasses?" Or I will make a simple comment, such as "That's really interesting." And I'm going to tell myself it's OK to be quiet for a while.

Now go ahead and describe some of your own situations where you need some time to adjust. Follow up by listing at least one warm-up strategy for each situation:

Situation 1: _____

Warm-up strategy: _____

_____

_____

Situation 2: _____

Warm-up strategy: _____

_____

_____

Situation 3: _____

Warm-up strategy: _____

_____

_____

Voices

"One of my best friends told me that she used to think I was a know-it-all snob. She said I never said hello to her in the halls or talked to her in class. We didn't get to know each other until we worked on the play together. The reason I didn't say hello to her or anybody else is that I felt too shy. But working on the play gave us lots of time to be around each other, and after a few days I felt relaxed enough to talk to her."

—Hannah, a high school junior

"I have a pretty good sense of humor, but most people don't know it. I just don't feel comfortable telling jokes or teasing people until I know them really well. Sometimes that really bothers me. I wish I could be one of those funny guys that everybody likes right away. But I'm not. It doesn't bother me as much now as it used to. It just takes me a little while to feel OK enough to joke around. And that's the way it is."

—Lamar, a college freshman

Journal

Think of a regular event that you would like to participate in but usually don't because you feel too shy. Talk a little about that event and what makes you feel uncomfortable in that situation. Then think of several things you could do to give yourself more time to warm up.

Event I want to participate in:

_____

_____

_____

_____

Why I think I'll be uncomfortable if I go:

_____

_____

_____

_____

What I could do to give myself more time to warm up:

_____

_____

_____

_____

DAY 6   What Is Your Comfort Zone?

What You Need to Know

Most teens like to have some places, social situations, and activities where they feel completely comfortable. Shy teens seek out comfort zones that will help them feel safe—zones where they can be free to be themselves and not be shy. The following are examples of such comfort zones:

> **Physical Comfort Zones**—Being in various places where you can feel calm and comfortable (for example, your bedroom, the beanbag chair in your basement, the library, the band room)

> **Social Comfort Zones**—Being with people who make you feel comfortable (for example, certain family members, a few close friends, a particular teacher)

> **Personal Comfort Zones**—Taking part in activities that you feel confident doing (for example, strumming a guitar, reading, playing video games, skateboarding)

There is nothing wrong with having comfort zones. Shy teens, however, often become so intent on finding security in these comfort zones that the zones essentially become hiding places where the teens know they can go when they begin to feel anxious or overwhelmed. As a result, these comfort zones can become places that the shy teens depend on to such an extent that they are not willing to change their habits when the anxiety becomes too much for them— or when they *think* the anxiety is becoming too much for them. Sometimes these comfort zones continue to shrink as the shy teens reflexively retreat to places, groups, and activities that they perceive as presenting no risk to them.

Relying too heavily on and remaining in their comfort zones can make shy teens less likely to take social risks. But if shy teens become aware of the comfort zones, these comfort zones can become bases from which they can venture out and take risks. For example, a shy teen might have a group of good friends with whom she feels comfortable. When the teen wants to go to a new place, she can ask the group to go with her. This lets her use the social comfort she feels with her friends to expand her physical comfort zone.

Understanding comfort zones is another way of understanding shyness. Eventually, understanding this relationship helps shy teens develop strategies for dealing successfully with their shyness.

Your Turn

List your comfort zones in each of the following areas. Try to describe
what makes you feel safe in each of these zones.

My Physical Comfort Zones (Specific Places)

_____

_____

_____

_____

My Social Comfort Zones (Individuals or Groups of People)

_____

_____

_____

_____

My Personal Comfort Zones (Activities)

_____

_____

_____

_____

Voices

"I have a big family, and we live in a small apartment, so I don't have much space to myself. But at night, after everyone else has gone to bed, I can curl up in this old wicker chair in the corner of the kitchen and read or draw or listen to my music on headphones. It's just my place to be me."

—Winnie, a seventh-grade student

"There aren't many people I can be myself with. I have one friend who has known me since second grade. I guess she knows how I am about everything. And somehow she still likes me. She's the only person I feel totally comfortable around all the time."

—Shana, a ninth-grade student

"At church I sing in the youth choir. We practice twice a week and sing during two services on Sunday. I feel so good when I'm singing, and I love lifting my voice in praise. I just feel so alive. The director doesn't put up with any nonsense and gives lots of compliments, so practices are super-smooth. And as a treat, sometimes we have cake or ice cream after practice. I wish I could go to choir every single day."

—Malcolm, a 10th-grade student

Journal

Describe a comfort zone where you often hide to escape from bad feelings. Keep in mind that this can be a place, a relationship, or an activity. *(If you want to, feel free to describe other comfort zones where you hide.)*

1. Which comfort zone do you often use?

_____

_____

_____

_____

2. What causes you to hide there?

_____

_____

_____

_____

3. What is one thing you could do to stop hiding in that comfort zone?

_____

_____

_____

_____

DAY 7   How You Feel about Yourself

What You Need to Know

How you feel about yourself is often called *self-esteem.* You might hear somebody say, "Oh, she has such low self-esteem," which means she doesn't seem to think much of herself. But self-esteem isn't usually an all-or-nothing proposition. Each of us has things we think we do well and things we think we don't do well.

When some of the things that shy individuals think they don't do well relate to areas that affect how they deal with their shyness, then their low self-esteem can make it difficult to be successfully shy. For instance:

> *Paul would like to be able to talk to people he doesn't know well in social situations, but he thinks he is lousy at making small talk.*

> *Wendy would like to go to some of the school dances, but she thinks she looks funny when she dances.*

On the other hand, if a shy teen thinks he doesn't do something well—yet the reason he doesn't do something well really has nothing to do with his shyness—then low self-esteem for his perceived lack of skill will have no bearing on his being successfully shy. For instance:

> *David has low self-esteem about math, but this doesn't really have any effect on his shyness.*

As these examples illustrate, what is most telling about the relationship between self-esteem and shyness is how one feels about oneself in areas *directly relating* to one's interaction in social situations.

Your Turn

To help you evaluate how your shyness relates to your self-esteem, list eight skills you possess that make it possible for you to be comfortable with others:

1. _____   5. _____

2. _____   6. _____

3. _____   7. _____

4. _____   8. _____

Now list eight skills you wish you possessed that would help you to be comfortable in social situations:

1. _____   5. _____

2. _____   6. _____

3. _____   7. _____

4. _____   8. _____

Voices

"I wish I could play guitar or piano or drums. People who can play music always have something they can do at parties. I tried to learn to play guitar once. I gave up after a month because my fingers got sore and I never understood how to strum. It looks so easy when other people are doing it. I just don't have any talent."

—Brian, a high school junior

"Most of the time I feel pretty lousy about myself. I don't have many friends, and I sit at home on the weekends. My mom keeps saying that I make good grades in school and that's all that's important. But it doesn't feel that way. I don't want to spend my life in a library."

—DeLeisha, a high school senior

Journal

Look back at the list you made of eight skills you possess that help you in social situations and eight skills you wished you possessed, and consider these questions:

What was harder for you to list—the things you can do or the things you wish you could do? Why?

_____

_____

_____

_____

_____

_____

When looking at the two lists, how important is each skill in helping you deal with your shyness? Is there a tendency for you to value the skills in one list more than the skills in the other list? If so, why?

_____

_____

_____

_____

_____

_____

DAY 8 What Makes You Shy?

What You Need to Know

Shyness is different for each individual. Luke and Bob both describe themselves as shy individuals, but their shyness presents itself in different ways. When they walk into a roomful of strangers, Luke feels shy and Bob does not. On the other hand, when it comes to answering a question aloud in class, Bob feels shy and Luke does not.

It is also true that shyness creates different types of problems for different people. For instance, both Lucia and Ramona would like to be able to talk to new people without getting tongue-tied and sweaty and scared. But Lucia's family has moved a number of times, causing Lucia to attend one or two new schools each year. So it's no surprise that talking to new people is a big problem for her. Ramona, meanwhile, has lived in the same town all her life. Although she is shy, people know her and are aware that she takes a little time to feel comfortable. They are patient with her, and therefore shyness is not as big a problem for her as it is for Lucia, unless of course Ramona goes away to college or leaves town for a new job.

It is important for shy teens to gain an understanding of their own reaction to the underlying dynamics (in other words, the process of change or growth) of their shyness. As a reminder, those dynamics, which have been the focus of the past three days of the workbook, are listed as follows:

✦ The approach-avoidance conflict
✦ The slow-to-warm-up tendency
✦ The comfort zone

When shy teens can combine these three dynamics with an understanding of their own self-esteem, they will be taking a big step toward dealing with their shyness. First, it will help to identify exactly what types of situations trigger their shyness.

Your Turn

Personal Shyness Inventory

Consider the following statements and answer them as completely as you can:

1. Describe any factors you believe have contributed to your shyness:

   _____

   _____

2. Describe how your shyness is expressed (for example, through an inability to talk, clumsiness, avoidance of new situations):

   _____

   _____

3. Describe the problems your shyness has created in your life:

   _____

   _____

4. Describe what you have done to overcome your shyness:

   _____

   _____

Voices

"I hate junior high. There are all these people in the halls and at lunch that I don't know. I mean, I've been here three months, and I still mix up the names of lots of the people in my classes. I used to feel so happy in my elementary school. We stayed with the same teacher all day and I knew everybody. Now my friends are in different classes and I never see them. And high school is going to be twice as many people as junior high. I hate it already."

—Tim, a seventh-grade student

"I think I started feeling shy when I was about 10. When I came back to school in fifth grade, I was taller than everybody else, and my body had changed in other ways, too. Some of the boys that used to talk to me started laughing at me behind my back and saying nasty things about me. I started staying inside at recess to help the teacher, instead of going outside where people would laugh at me. Even though everybody has caught up to me now in size and stuff, I still remember how bad that hurt. It changed me forever."

—Esperanza, a sophomore student

Journal

Write about the time your shyness caused you the greatest problem.
What happened? What did you feel? How has that incident affected you?

_____

_____

_____

_____

_____

_____

_____

_____

_____

_____

_____

_____

_____

_____

DAY 9　Taking Control of Your Shyness

What You Need to Know

Do shy teens need to change who they are to become successfully shy? The answer clearly is no. There is nothing wrong with being shy. To be *successfully* shy requires that shy teens change what they think and what they do, not who they are.

To be successfully shy, shy teens need to be in control of their shyness rather than vice versa. To take control of their shyness, shy teens first need to understand the situations that make them feel shy and continue from that point.

Next, shy teens have to set a series of clear goals en route to becoming successfully shy. As we saw in Days 7 and 8, shy teens sometimes see shyness as one major hurdle. This perception, however, makes it more difficult for them to solve their shyness problem because it's especially difficult to attack a problem if it is viewed as one monumental obstacle. If shyness—the principal problem that needs to be solved—is broken down into a number of smaller problems, the task of teenagers becomes a lot easier because now all they have to do is to fit several smaller pieces to complete the puzzle. By using such an approach, shy teens will be on their way to dealing successfully with their shyness.

Your Turn

When dealing with shyness, it is helpful to set specific goals. Look back at the previous eight days and read what you wrote about the different problems that your shyness causes you. Pay special attention to the situations that you indicated you would like to improve.

Now you are ready to set some "general goals" for yourself. A general goal identifies a skill that's used in a variety of situations that cover a lot of ground and can therefore be lumped together. For instance, Lin wants to feel comfortable talking to people she doesn't know well. Hers is a general goal that can cover many different situations. The catalyst, or motivation, for her needing to set a general goal is her wish to be able to feel comfortable talking with her lab partner in science class. That smaller goal is not a general goal but rather a goal that deals with a specific situation.

To begin, identify no more than two general goals and then list some current situations in which you want to apply those goals. In Lin's case, the three situations she would like to work on under her general goal are (a) talking to her lab partner, (b) talking to the new family in her neighborhood, and (c) talking to people at parties.

General goal 1: _____

Specific situations: _____

_____

_____

General goal 2: _____

Specific situations: _____

_____

_____

Voices

"I would like to be able to go on a date with somebody and be able to talk and have fun. I usually feel so uncomfortable and I never know what to say or how to act. I'm not surprised that nobody ever asks me out again."

—Diana, an 18-year-old community college student

"I have a few summer job interviews coming up. I'm usually OK with some of the questions, but there are always a lot of questions I don't feel comfortable with. And sometimes they just want you to talk about yourself, and they don't ask any questions at all. I hate that! I just wish I could be more comfortable talking about myself during these interviews."

—Felipe, a 16-year-old high school student

"I keep telling myself that I am going to do a better job of talking in my classes. Most of my teachers give points for class participation. But it takes me so long to decide to answer a question that somebody else has already tried to answer, and they are on the next question before I even raise my hand. And I know the answer!"

—Willa, an eighth-grade student

Journal

Reread the general goals and specific situations that you listed in this lesson's (Day 9's) "Your Turn" section. Now select those specific situations that are most important to you. Write about why it is critical for you to be more in control of your shyness in those situations than in the others.

_____

_____

_____

_____

_____

_____

_____

_____

_____

_____

_____

_____

_____

_____

Part III

Strategies for Successfully Shy Teens

DAY 10   Understanding the Role of Anxiety

What You Need to Know

Before you start working on your shyness goals, it is important to clear up some misunderstandings about anxiety. Most shy teens describe anxiety as the major obstacle that stops them from doing something they want to do. They mention having butterflies, sweaty palms, dry mouth, or being tongue-tied as evidence that they feel anxious.

But anxiety really happens because you see a situation as threatening. Either there is a real danger, or in most cases you are imagining that there is a danger. In some situations, anxiety alerts you to a threat and can save your life. For instance, say you are outside and hear thunder. You realize there is a potential danger in remaining outside and feel anxious, and this anxiety pushes you to go inside to a safe place until the storm has passed. The anxiety has thus helped you to cope with a dangerous situation.

The shy mind has a different kind of problem with anxiety. Instead of heeding the warning and using a good coping strategy to relieve the anxiety, the shy mind focuses on the anxiety rather than on the threat. The shy teen with the shy mind somehow gets stuck in the feeling of anxiety and doesn't make a move to deal with the real or imagined threat. For instance, when Carlo prepares to attend the first day of football practice at his new high school, he is afraid that he will be ignored or laughed at by the other kids. When he actually gets to the practice field, he finds himself thinking so much about his own anxiety that he is unable to do anything to help himself feel at ease. He withdraws into himself, making it even more unlikely that the other players will talk to him. Carlo's anxiety also makes it hard for him to perform well, to do his best.

Your Turn

Look back at the situations that you listed under your two goals in Day 9. Which of these situations create anxiety for you? (Mark any such situations with an A in the margin.)

Now take two of these situations and identify the threat you feel for each. Describe how your feelings of anxiety prevent you from dealing with both situations.

Sample situation: Carlo wants to feel comfortable on the first day of football practice.
Threat: Carlo fears that the other players will ignore him or laugh at him.
What anxiety does: Anxiety prevents Carlo from being able to smile or laugh or joke around or be able to do well at practice.

Situation 1: _____

_____

Threat: _____

_____

What anxiety does: _____

_____

Situation 2: _____

_____

Threat: _____

_____

What anxiety does: _____

_____

Voices

"I went on my first date with Maura last week. We'd been friends for a while, and it didn't seem like too big a deal to take her to the dance after the game. It's pretty lame to show up there without a date. I figured I'd be OK because we knew each other so well. But when I was walking to the car with her, I just got so anxious. It was as if I'd never seen her before. What if she didn't like me as a date, just as a friend, and ditched me once we got to the dance? I didn't say a word the whole trip to the dance, and things went downhill from there."

—Isaiah, a high school junior

"We have a talent show at our school that is always a lot of fun to watch. My friends have been trying to get me to audition for two years. So this year I finally did. I figured, what could it hurt? My chorus teacher was one of the judges, and he has always liked my voice. But while I was waiting offstage, I got so anxious, my stomach was tied in knots and I started shaking when I talked. I almost didn't make it across the stage when they called my name. I kept thinking about how awful some of the other kids sounded. What if my friends were wrong? What if I wasn't any good? I was so scared when the piano was playing my intro that my first note was a croak. I just rushed off the stage without finishing."

—Bette, an eighth-grade student

Journal

Read back over the two situations that you listed in the "Your Turn" section today (Day 10) that make you anxious. Try to identify at least one thing you could have done in each situation instead of thinking so much about your anxiety.

_____

_____

_____

_____

_____

_____

_____

_____

_____

_____

_____

_____

_____

_____

_____

_____

DAY 11   Alcohol Is Not the Answer

What You Need to Know

When shy individuals get anxious, they often look for easy ways to deal with that anxiety. Instead of trying to understand the threat and deal with it, the shy mind looks for some other way to cope with anxiety. One thing some teens do is to use alcohol.

Does alcohol make you less anxious?

Yes, it can. Alcohol is a depressant of the nervous system, which means you are less likely to be aroused or nervous when drinking alcohol.

Does alcohol help you deal with your shyness?

No, it doesn't. Although alcohol can help you feel a little less anxious at first, it also slows down your mental processes. Alcohol makes it harder for you to use the strategies you are learning in this workbook to deal with your shyness.

Shy individuals think their anxiety will be reduced if they have a drink at a social event where they feel uncomfortable. Even though alcohol is illegal for teens, there are still many social events where it is available. Some teens think they will relax after a drink and won't feel as anxious.

Teens sometimes feel more accepted if they drink like everyone else. But the problem is that you have to drink even more each time to get accepted and feel more relaxed.

Another negative aspect of their turning to alcohol for help is that, more often than not, shy teens find themselves in situations in which they do not have access to alcohol, for instance, at school. If you think that alcohol is the only way to deal with your shyness, you will end up with other, much bigger problems. That's because some teens do try to sneak a drink from their locker before going into a situation where they feel shy. And that signals a "trouble alert."

Using the strategies in this workbook to become successfully shy is much more effective and won't have the harmful side effects of using alcohol to deal with your shyness.

Your Turn

What are the silliest things you've seen people do when they are drinking alcohol? What are the most disgusting things you've seen people do when they are drinking alcohol?

Silliest: _____

_____

_____

_____

_____

_____

_____

Most disgusting: _____

_____

_____

_____

_____

_____

_____

Voices

"Man, I hate walking into a party and not knowing anybody. People everywhere, and they all seem to be having a good time except you. That's why I like to have a drink as soon as I get to a party. It makes me feel mellow. I don't care if nobody talks to me. After a few drinks I'll talk to them and I'm having a great time. Of course I get some weird looks the next day. But so what? I don't feel shy at all, and that's the most important thing."

—Ted, a high school junior

"I used to drink when I went out with my friends. I've got a cool bunch of friends, and lots of times I don't really have much to say. I know they just included me because they had known me forever. So I would have something to drink before I left the house, and then I would have some beers that somebody had brought along. It made me feel relaxed and happy and I didn't worry so much. But one day, Sandy told me that everybody liked me better when I wasn't drinking. She said they didn't care if I was quiet, just so I was me. When I was drinking, they couldn't tell what I'd be like. It was like they were with a stranger."

—Mookie, a high school freshman

Journal

Describe two situations in which you or someone you know has used alcohol to try to deal with shyness. What happened in both cases?

Situation 1: _____

_____

_____

_____

_____

_____

_____

_____

Situation 2: _____

_____

_____

_____

_____

_____

_____

_____

DAY 12　Strategies for Controlling Your Anxiety: Part I

What You Need to Know

You may find this surprising, but it's actually a *good* thing to feel some anxiety as part of your shyness. How can that be? Well, if you are anxious, it means you are stepping outside your comfort zone and trying something new. So feeling anxious means you are being brave as well as anxious. *(Be sure to give yourself a pat on the back!)*

But you don't want to focus on your anxiety so much that you aren't able to do anything. So what do you do? Here are four easy steps you can use for dealing with your anxiety, followed by a scenario that shows the four steps in action:

Step 1: Tell yourself it's OK to be anxious. (Remember what was just discussed: You are being brave because you're outside your comfort zone.) It's normal to be a little anxious.

Step 2: Take your anxiety temperature. Are you just a little above normal, suffering from merely a slight anxiety fever? Great. You can cope with that. What if you are feeling a lot of anxiety? That's still OK, but only if you slow down and give yourself time to get calm. If your anxiety temperature is off the charts, maybe it's a signal for you to back off and try this another time—after you've analyzed what freaked you out.

Step 3: Unless you *are* freaked out, slow down and try to see what the threat is. What are you afraid might happen? Now try to figure out how likely it is that it will happen. If the worst does happen, can you live with it?

Step 4: Give yourself time and be patient. Because you are shy, it takes you a while to warm up. Instead of running away, try to stick around and give yourself time to feel more comfortable.

Scenario

*Lucinda is shopping at the mall with her best friend, Chris. After a few minutes, they run into some other girls from their class. Chris suggests they all shop together. Lucinda becomes very anxious and almost leaves. But she tells herself it's OK to be anxious; after all, she didn't expect this to happen (**Step 1**). Lucinda takes her anxiety temperature and finds that she is pretty uncomfortable, but not totally* panicked *(Step 2)*. She tries to figure out the threat. Maybe Chris won't talk to her at all and will only talk to the other girls *(Step 3)*. The more she thinks about that possibility, though, the less she thinks it likely to happen. After all, Chris is her friend—her *best* friend. Lucinda decides to wait about 20 minutes or so and then take a fresh look at how things are going. She can then make a better, more informed decision whether to stay or go *(Step 4)*.

Your Turn

Describe a time recently when you got really anxious in a new situation. Go through each of the four steps and analyze your anxiety.

Situation: _____

Step 1: What did you tell yourself about your anxiety?

_____

_____

Step 2: What was your anxiety temperature?

_____

_____

Step 3: What was the threat? What were you afraid might happen?

_____

_____

Step 4: How could you have stayed in the situation longer to give yourself more time to get comfortable?

_____

_____

What did you actually do? Did using the four steps make a difference in your decision?

_____

_____

Voices

"My brother is a year older than me. I like to hang around with him. He had some friends over to play basketball in our driveway. I knew some of them. Some I didn't. I was afraid they wouldn't want me to play. I just went inside."

—Pete, a 12-year-old

"I joined a service club that meets on Saturday. We take a bus someplace to help with a project. Like sorting food at Dare to Care. I like the work we do because it makes me feel good. But different people show up every week. I know one or two people I can talk to, but sometimes they don't come. Then I feel really uncomfortable. It gets better once we start working, but it takes me a long time to feel OK."

—Marian, a 14-year-old

Journal

Write about a time when you were really anxious in a new situation, but instead of leaving, you stayed and things went really well in spite of your anxiety. Write about some of the things you did to pass the time until you felt less anxious.

_____

_____

_____

_____

_____

_____

_____

_____

_____

_____

_____

_____

_____

_____

DAY 13 Strategies for Controlling Your Anxiety: Part II

What You Need to Know

Now that you have followed the four steps for analyzing your anxiety and you've stayed in the situation, you've allowed yourself to get comfortable and things have gone OK. How can you build on this success?

Do you recall hearing this old joke?

Question: How do you get to Carnegie Hall?

Answer: Practice, practice, practice.

Well, that's what you do to control your anxiety: You *practice* the same behavior again and again.

Let's look again at Carlo, who was anxious about the first day of football practice. What if he used the four steps for analyzing his anxiety and gave himself time to feel comfortable? The following is a much likelier scenario than the one he experienced earlier:

Carlo says something to the people standing next to him, and every-thing is working out OK. In 15–20 minutes or so, he says something else. He continues to do this throughout practice. Each time, he says just a couple of words, but he doesn't clam up the way he did before. And then every time he says something—a little bit here, a little bit there—and continues in this manner, he begins to feel less and less anxious.

In addition to *practice,* the other key to controlling your anxiety is *persistence.* Suppose you take your anxiety temperature when you walk into a roomful of strangers and decide you are freaked out. You leave. That's OK. Sometimes you can be too anxious to take something on as soon as you're faced with it. But then you use the four steps to analyze what happened, and the next day or the next week, you go back and try again. This time you feel a little more comfortable, and so you stay for a while longer than you would have previously. Maybe you don't say anything, but nonetheless you stay. The next time you stay longer and actually say something. Remember the two keys—the two **P**s—that will help you control your anxiety: **P**ractice and **P**ersistence.

Your Turn

Look again at the situation you wrote about in Day 12 (or if you prefer, choose a different situation). Answer the following questions to see exactly how you could have applied the two Ps—Practice and Persistence—when you felt anxious in this particular situation.

What can you do to feel more comfortable in this situation?

_____

_____

_____

How can you **practice** your solutions from above in other situations?

_____

_____

_____

What can you do the next time this situation occurs?

_____

_____

_____

What other opportunities **(persistence)** will enable you to practice your new solutions?

_____

_____

_____

_____

Voices

"When I go to Pep Club meetings, I am usually very quiet. There are a lot of people who talk a lot. I never have anything good to say. I do like working on the posters for the games. I started talking to the girl I was working with on a poster. I just said a couple of things about the colors we were using or something dumb. But she agreed. So I said something else. Before I knew it, we were talking to each other. It felt great. Next week I'm going to try talking to her again."

—Linda, a high school sophomore

"I sit with the same people at lunch every day. But I talk mostly to Ron. We're into the same kind of video games. If he's not there, I don't talk much. But he broke his leg and was at home for a week. By the third day, I was tired of being quiet. So I asked one of the other guys what video games he played. We talked a little. Then I asked somebody else. The next day a guy brought in a gaming magazine, and we all looked at it. Lunch zoomed by. When Ron came back, he was really surprised. I was talking to everybody."

—Jack, a 13-year-old

Journal

Write about any experiences you've had in which practice or persist-ence paid off. Your topic doesn't have to be about shyness. It can be about anything that turned out better because you practiced and persisted.

_____

_____

_____

_____

_____

_____

_____

_____

_____

_____

_____

_____

_____

_____

_____

DAY 14   I Can't Get It out of My Head

What You Need to Know

Let's listen in on Joey's thoughts as he enters the school building:

> *I can't believe my bus got here this early. What am I going to do for*
> *15 minutes? I can kill some time at my locker, but then what? Nobody*
> *is going to talk to me. Even if somebody does have a brain glitch and*
> *says hello to me, I won't know what to say back. I wonder if I can find*
> *someplace to hide so people won't see what a loser I am.*

Does any of that sound familiar?

Shy individuals say a lot of things to themselves that keep them from dealing with their shyness. The things they tell themselves are not helpful. We call this behavior "shyness of the mind," and it is present in most shy people.

How can you get these negative thoughts out of your head? That's what you're going to work on for the next three days. By understanding your shy thoughts, you will be better able to deal with them.

Your Turn

By looking at Joey's thoughts as he arrives at school, we can imagine a number of other thoughts that are running around in his head.

"Nobody will talk to me."

"I won't know what to say."

"I'm a loser."

There's one more thought that he doesn't say directly, but that is really at the bottom of all of this negativity: "Everyone else has somebody to talk to, except me. Everyone else would know what to say, except me."

What are the most common thoughts that are running around in your head when you feel shy? List as many of them as you can identify:

_____

_____

_____

_____

_____

_____

_____

_____

_____

_____

_____

Voices

"I heard the new kid telling people he's a skateboarder. That's my favorite thing to do. I'd love to talk to him, but I don't know what to say. I'd just sound stupid. Then he'll think I'm an idiot and never talk to me. I'll wear my skateboard shirt tomorrow. Maybe he'll notice it and say something to me."

—Tony, a seventh-grade student

"The PE teacher asked for volunteers to work the concession stand at the ball game this weekend. It doesn't pay anything, but you get free popcorn and a drink when your shift is finished. I think I'd like to do it. But what if I have to talk to a lot of people I don't know? I probably wouldn't know what to say. People would think I was an idiot. If I knew I could stay in the background, I'd volunteer for sure. I wonder if they could use somebody who just cooks the hot dogs and doesn't have to talk."

—Marisa, a 14-year-old student

Journal

Some of the negative thoughts that run around in the shy mind start as comments made by other people. Write about any times that other people have identified you as somebody who couldn't do something because you were too shy.

_____

_____

_____

_____

_____

_____

_____

_____

_____

_____

_____

_____

_____

_____

DAY 15   It's All about Me

What You Need to Know

The shy mind can play tricks on you. When you are in a new or uncomfortable situation, your mind will trick you by telling you something like this: "Everyone is looking at me. Everyone is waiting for me to mess up."

How wrong that is. Even people who aren't shy are *usually* thinking about themselves and not about other people. They want to be sure they are looking good, sounding cool, and not messing up.

Your shy mind is telling you something quite different. Your shy mind is telling you that *everyone* is looking at you. And that makes you even more uncomfortable.

So how do you deal with this self-consciousness? Here are some tips you can use:

1. Tell yourself it's OK to feel uncomfortable. It doesn't mean you are weird—just that you are not comfortable yet.

2. Do something small to stop thinking about yourself. Say hello to someone, go get a soft drink, sit down, just watch the scene for a while.

3. Change what you are thinking. Keep telling yourself, "People care more about what *they* are doing than what *I* am doing." (By the way, there is one good thing about being shy. It's unlikely that you *are* going to do something really stupid like standing on your head and singing the national anthem. In a case like that, everyone would be looking at you for sure.)

4. Remain calm and use the other skills you've learned to deal with shyness, such as giving yourself time to warm up and feel comfortable. And remember, nobody is even going to notice that you're having trouble being in an unfamiliar situation. They are too busy looking at themselves.

Your Turn

Test this out: Put yourself in a situation that you think might make you uncomfortable, such as talking to somebody you haven't talked to before, sitting with people you don't know very well, asking a clerk a question at the mall, and so forth.

What is your mind telling you?

Now look around. What evidence do you have that everyone is looking at you?

Do one thing instead of thinking about yourself. What did you do?

While waiting to warm up, write down a few positive messages you can give yourself.

_____

_____

_____

_____

_____

_____

_____

_____

_____

_____

Voices

"I went to my cousin's birthday party last week. He's my age, but we don't have any of the same friends. I knew it was a mistake as soon as I walked in the door. They were all looking at me like, 'What are you doing here? You don't belong.' I was miserable. I left as soon as I could."

—Tina, a 15-year-old

"I'm failing math. My math teacher offered to tutor me after school. I did it once, but never again. All those kids walking by the door knew why I was there. I know they think I'm too stupid to get math without help. I couldn't stand their looks of pity. I'd rather fail math."

—Mike, a 13-year-old student

Journal

Write about a time you recall feeling very self-conscious. What was the situation, and what did your shy mind tell you?

_____

_____

_____

_____

_____

_____

_____

_____

_____

_____

_____

_____

_____

_____

_____

DAY 16   Everybody Makes Mistakes

What You Need to Know

The shy mind can play all kinds of tricks on you. Let's look at what happened to Gary:

> Gary went to a party with a couple of friends, but when he got there, he didn't know anyone else. His friends knew a few people and seemed OK, but Gary almost left. His shy mind told him that everyone would be watching him, waiting to see what he would do. But Gary decided to stay for a while. He got a soft drink, stood in a corner so he could watch what was going on, and told himself he was going to relax. So far, so good. Then a couple of girls came over to talk to him. They asked him what TV shows he liked, and he answered, "Anything about sports, especially football and basketball." One girl said, "Oh, yuck. Another jock. How boring." After a minute, they both walked off.

Question: What does Gary's shy mind tell him about what just happened?

a. "Maybe I shouldn't have mentioned sports. A lot of girls don't like sports."

b. "I should have asked them what kind of TV they like."

c. "I'm so stupid! I should have known not to talk about sports."

Answer: Gary's shy mind tells him all three: a, b, and c. In fact, it tells him answer c over and over again!

The shy mind makes you think everything you do is a mistake. It doesn't give you a break. The shy mind makes a big deal out of something that is just an everyday occurrence. In reality, there was nothing at all wrong with what Gary said. He didn't make a mistake. Those girls simply didn't like sports. In fact, the chances were just as good that another pair of girls would've reacted differently and joined Gary in a discussion about sports shows. The problem was that Gary's shy mind told him he had made a big mistake, and so he left the party.

It's important for a shy person to realize that one bad interaction doesn't mean the whole scene is bad. Gary needs to cut himself a break and try again.

Your Turn

Instead of listening to your shy mind tell you what an idiot you've been, try substituting some messages that say just the opposite. Here are some examples:

✦ It's no big deal.

✦ That could have happened to anybody.

✦ So what?

✦ Most of the time, I do the right thing.

Now come up with some things to say that make your mistake seem less awful to you.

_____

_____

_____

_____

_____

_____

_____

_____

_____

_____

_____

Voices

"I was at a party and was talking to some people. There was a boy I really liked talking to. I really felt comfortable with him. I thought he said his name was Tim, but I later found out it was Tad. I guess I just didn't hear him with all the noise. I called him the wrong name all night. He must think I'm an idiot. He left me a message on my cell, but no way I called him back."

—Elise, a high school junior

"I was working at the yard sale at our church. It's something I do every year, and it's a lot of fun. I know a lot of the people, and I just put people's stuff in a plastic bag while they are paying for it. I don't have to say much. I just smile and say, "Thank you for supporting St. Barnabas." Well, I looked up to say that, and the face looking back at me was this guy from school I have a crush on. I couldn't think of anything to say, and so I blurted out, "Thank you for supporting Jeanie." I mean, how stupid was that? He smiled at me, but I never ever want to see him again. I've got to figure out a way not to run into him at school."

—Jeanie, a 13-year-old

"We always have a lot of family and friends over for Thanksgiving dinner. This year I stumbled and dropped a Jell-O salad on the floor. It was a sticky mess. I felt so clumsy and stupid. But my mom told everybody about the time she dropped the turkey when she was taking it to the table. Then somebody else had another story about dropping a cake and getting icing all over the carpet. Pretty soon I could see that what I did really was no big deal."

—Dwayne, a 16-year-old

Journal

Write about a time that you were out of your comfort zone and tried a new activity, but then something went wrong. What did your shy mind tell you about your mistake? What messages could you have substituted to make your mistake seem more acceptable?

DAY 17   Playing the Blame Game

What You Need to Know

When something happens to us, we want to understand why it happened. We want an explanation. Let's go back and look at Gary, who went to the party and was just standing in the corner, drinking his soda. At first nobody was talking to him. Maybe Gary wondered, "Why isn't anybody talking to me?"

Because Gary is a shy individual, his shy mind likely came up with the following explanation: "Nobody is talking to me because I am boring and nobody is interested in me." Thus Gary assumes that he, and he alone, is totally to blame. He also takes it a step further by thinking: "Nobody is talking to me now, and nobody is going to want to talk to me the entire night because I am such a boring person."

Wow! Gary's setting up a pretty grim scenario, and according to him, it is *all* his fault. But Gary's shy mind isn't finished, as the following thought haunts him: "There's not a party in the world I could walk into and find somebody who would want to talk to me because I'm such a boring person."

Doom and gloom. But that is how the shy mind works. Gary is accepting all the blame and is taking it all personally. That's a great way to destroy his self-confidence.

Your Turn

Look back at Gary's situation. He is at a party, standing in the corner, and nobody is talking to him. The truth is, Gary is an interesting person. The ideas he's saying to himself—the reasons his shy mind gives for his alienation from the crowd—are wrong. Now list all the reasons you can think of to explain why people aren't talking to him.

Voices

"I finally got up the courage to say something in class the other day, and somebody disagreed with me. The teacher didn't say I was wrong, but she didn't say I was right. I'm sure I must have been wrong. It was a stupid opinion. Nobody needs to know what I think. I'll never say anything people will want to hear. Everybody would be happier if I just shut up."

—DeShane, a high school sophomore

"I interviewed to be an aide in the school library, and the librarian asked me lots of questions about the kinds of books I like to read. I couldn't think of the names of some of the books. And if I knew the name of the book, I couldn't think of the name of the author. I felt really dumb. I bet she's never had anybody that dumb try to be an aide before. Now I don't even want to go into the library. And I'll never, ever try to get another job."

—Bebe, an eighth-grade student

Journal

Describe a situation where you felt really shy. If you want to, you can refer to a time you've already written about on another day. Now list the various ways that you blamed yourself for what happened. At the end of your description of the incident, list some other possible explanations for what happened that had nothing to do with you.

Situation: _____

_____

How I blamed myself: _____

_____

Other reasons things might have gone wrong that had nothing to do with me:

_____

_____

_____

_____

_____

_____

_____

_____

_____

_____

DAY 18   Credit Where Credit Is Due: Who, Me?

What You Need to Know

There is another side to the blame game, and here is an example:

> *Shauna joins a club at school during activity period. At the first meeting she feels pretty uncomfortable, and nobody really talks to her. But at the second meeting, two girls sitting near her start talking about a new CD they like. Shauna bought this CD, too, and she starts talking about the songs she likes. The three girls have a lot of fun, and Shauna feels more comfortable.*

So what's the problem? Here's how the conversation goes inside Shauna's shy mind:

> *Wow! Wasn't I lucky that I happened to have the same CD as those girls. And I was even luckier that they let me talk to them. And I was luckiest that they were nice girls. They were probably the only nice girls in the club. And those girls are too nice to ever want to talk to me again.*

Do you hear what is happening in Shauna's mind? She had a good experience and thinks it is due to luck alone. She doesn't give herself any credit at all. In addition, she thinks nothing that good will happen to her again. So let's look at what Shauna *did* say and do:

1. She likes music.
2. She is able to talk about the music she likes.
3. She is aware that others enjoy hearing what she has to say.
4. She is able to take turns talking. She doesn't monopolize conversations.
5. She listens to what other people have to say about music.

These are all things that Shauna did. And it is likely that other girls out there would see and do exactly the same things. Regrettably, Shauna isn't going to feel good about what happened because her shy mind took over and wouldn't allow her to take any credit.

Your Turn

Think of a time when you stepped outside your comfort zone and things went well. (If you want to, you can use the situation you talked about in your journal on Day 17.)

1. List three things you did to make things go well:

    a. _____

    b. _____

    c. _____

2. Name the different types of people you were with (high school kids, family, team members, and others):

    _____

    _____

3. Write down all the good things you can recall about the people you were with:

    _____

    _____

    (If you find that you're having difficulty with this exercise, keep in mind the trick to completing it successfully: Don't pay any attention to your shy mind.)

4. Now think of all the times in the future when it is likely that you will be around these same types of people again and have things go well. List *at least* three such future occasions.

    a. _____

    b. _____

    c. _____

    d. _____

Voices

"We were talking about the Civil War in history class last week. I go on reenactments with my family, so when we were talking about battles in our state, I raised my hand and told about a battlefield we had visited last week for a reenactment. People seemed really interested and asked what I wore and if I had a gun. Some people even kept talking to me in the hall and the next day. But that's the only interesting thing I do. We went on to something else in class, and of course I had absolutely nothing to say. I'm back to keeping my mouth shut."

—Liam, a 16-year-old female student

"My best friend talked me into working the tag sale at our school's Harvest Festival. We went the day before and helped price stuff that people donated. It was so much fun. There were all these crazy things people had donated, and we tried to guess what they were. I've never laughed so much and somehow I didn't feel shy. But something like that just happens once every million years. Too bad they don't have a tag sale every week."

—Marina, a 13-year-old student

Journal

Write about two times you actually enjoyed a social activity in spite of your shyness. Try to identify (and give yourself credit for) the things *you* did to make those activities successful for you.

1. _____

_____

_____

_____

_____

_____

_____

2. _____

_____

_____

_____

_____

_____

_____

DAY 19 Winning the Blame Game

What You Need to Know

If your shy mind is going to make you feel responsible when things don't go well while giving all the credit to other people when things do go well, how in the world are you going to win the blame game? To win, you will have to trick your shy mind. Here are two examples of how to trick your mind.

Sample Problem 1

Things *are not* going well.

Blame Game

"This is *all* my fault."

Trick

"Maybe only *some* of this is my fault."

Sample Problem 2

Things *are* going well.

Blame Game

"*None* of this success is because of me."

Trick

"Maybe *some* of this success is because of me."

Do you see what you need to do? Instead of letting your shy mind win, you are tricking it by saying maybe *some* of this is because of me, maybe *some* is not. This trick works either when things are going poorly or when things are going well.

Most important, you must give yourself a break. By giving yourself *some* credit for the problem and *some* credit for the success, you can stop the blame game.

Your Turn

Describe the following situations, as you have experienced them in your own life:

1. A social activity where you stepped out of your comfort zone and things did not go well.

   a. What the activity was, and what your shy mind said to blame yourself.

   b. One way in which some of the blame could have been due to where you were, the other people who were there, or something else that had nothing to do with you.

2. A social activity where you stepped out of your comfort zone and things went well.

   a. What the activity was, and what your shy mind said to give credit to somebody or something else for what went well.

   b. One way you could give some of the credit to yourself.

Voices

"OK. So I went to this ball game, see. And I was meeting some of my friends. But nobody showed. At first I was pretty mad. I figured they must have gone to do something else. They just didn't ask me. Or maybe it was all a setup. Maybe they were never coming. But maybe, just maybe, something happened. So I stayed at the game a little while. I just sat by myself. After 40 minutes, they showed up. Their car had a flat tire. Nobody knew how to change it. That's why it took them so long."

—Ricky, a 16-year-old

"I like books. I like to sit in the library and read where it's quiet. The librarian invited me to a book club, where kids talk about a book everyone reads. Most of the time I don't say anything. But one week they were talking about a book I love. So I said some things and some kids agreed with me. I was so surprised. I figured that would never happen again. But a few weeks later, I said something again. And kids started talking about what I said. Maybe I do have something to say sometimes."

—Mellie, a 14-year-old

Journal

Sometimes the blame game happens because shy people think that they have to be perfect. Write about some social situations in which you have felt the need to be perfect:

1. _____

_____

_____

_____

2. _____

_____

_____

_____

3. _____

_____

_____

_____

4. _____

_____

_____

_____

DAY 20   You're Better than I Am—Way Better!

What You Need to Know

Maurice went to the first dance of the year at his new school. Maurice is pretty shy and went to the dance only because some close friends were going. Although Maurice likes to dance at home when he is by himself, he hasn't done any dancing with people watching. So he stood on the sidelines and watched for a while. (Great strategy; it gave himself time to warm up and check out what was happening.)

But soon the floor cleared so everybody could watch J. J. dance. J. J. knew all the new moves and could make his body do amazing things. It didn't matter who he was dancing with—he looked terrific. Soon, other people went back on the floor, and Maurice's friends tried to get him to dance, but he said no.

"How can I get out there and dance? I'm not even close to being as good as J. J. and everybody would see that," Maurice told his friends. So he stayed on the sidelines and left early.

Shy teens often compare themselves to the very best person in the room. Whether it is dancing or talking or being popular, if you're a shy teen, you're only setting yourself up for failure when you choose the most talented person for comparison purposes. In time, it zaps your self-confidence and makes you feel even more and more shy.

Your Turn

Think about one of the situations you'd like to participate in, but that your shyness has made you uncomfortable with. Maybe you said to yourself, "If only I were like . . . ."

Whom do you wish you were like in this situation? Who is the star in your world? Who is the person you think has all the skills that you wish you had? List as many skills as you can think of that make this person a "star."

❏ 1. _____

❏ 2. _____

❏ 3. _____

❏ 4. _____

❏ 5. _____

❏ 6. _____

❏ 7. _____

❏ 8. _____

Now go back and put a check mark by any of the star's skills you listed that *you* also have. Insert the check mark even if you are only *moderately* skillful in that particular area, and not *tremendously* skillful.

Voices

"I just wish I could be like Shari. She has lots of friends. I mean, she's class president and a cheerleader and lots of other stuff. She always seems to have fun, even just standing in the hall. She's always smiling and has lots of people around her. But me, I'm just standing in the hall by myself or hiding in the bathroom."

—Marie, a high school freshman

"My brother keeps telling me I should go out for the cross-country team. He thinks I'm in pretty good shape and would like being on the team. But I won't ever do it. I was running around the school this summer, you know, just keeping in shape. The best runner on the team was out there, too. He blew me away like I was standing still. I'd be a total washout on that team. I'd get laughed off the road."

—Ray, a high school sophomore

Journal

Write about a time you wanted to do something, but somebody else was such a star that you got scared off. You thought you could never be that good, so you didn't do what you had wanted to do.

DAY 21   Find Somebody Your Own Size

What You Need to Know

Here are some things you can do to help your shy mind when you start to compare yourself to someone else:

1. Compare yourself to another individual only when the comparison has to do with something that is truly important to you. (Don't constantly compare yourself to others throughout the day.)

2. Pick someone who is like you in most ways, but has a skill that you admire.

3. Carefully study the skill the person has and see what you can learn. (You might even try talking to the person about his or her skill.)

Consider the following example:

Alisha wants to be in a play at school, but so far she has been too shy to audition. She has worked backstage on plays, but she dreams of being the star of the show, just like Tamara, who usually gets the big parts. Alisha knows that Tamara has been in plays since she was a little girl and has even taken acting and dancing lessons. Tamara has never worked backstage, though.

So Alisha decides to use her new "find somebody your own size" skills. She watches Keri, who has a small part with only a few lines. (Alisha met Keri last year when they both worked backstage.)

Being in a play is very important to Alisha, so she decides to talk to Keri for advice. Keri tells her that it wasn't hard to audition for this smaller role. All she did was talk to the drama teacher, and he helped her practice her lines. Keri said that last year she was in one play where she didn't have any lines at all, but she found the experience valuable because she got used to being on stage in front of all the people in the audience. Keri sounds as though she is shy in a similar way to Alisha. And Keri hasn't had any acting lessons, either. Alisha then decides to talk to the drama teacher about possibly getting a nonspeaking part in the next play.

Alisha changed her approach from making a comparison to a "star" to making a comparison to someone more like herself. This new strategy helped her find a way to make progress on her dream.

Your Turn

Think about something you would like to feel comfortable doing in front of people—playing the guitar, singing, playing pool, dancing, talking at a party, or something else. Once you decide on something you'd like to do, answer the following questions:

1. Who is the one person you know of who is best at doing the thing you would like to do most? This person should be someone you know—not some actor on TV or in the movies. (We'll call this person "The Star.")

2. What makes The Star so good at doing this?

3. In what ways is The Star like you? (You might compare criteria such as the neighborhoods you both live in, the kids you pal around with, your physical features, the style of clothes you wear, the grades you get, and so on.)

4. In what ways is The Star *not* like you?

Voices

"The thing I want to do most in the world is be in a band. I play drums. I'm not world class, but I'm OK. When I go to a concert, I just watch the drummer. But I could never figure out how to get from playing in my basement to being up there onstage. I just kept hoping somehow I'd get a chance. I have a friend, Roger, who plays guitar. We've known each other forever, and sometimes he'll come over and practice with me. He has the same dream about being in a band that I do. So one day we just decided to form our own band. We spread the word and had to turn people away who wanted to join. We just play at school dances and local stuff, mostly for free, but I can tell I'm getting a lot better, and so is Roger. I wish I had done this a long time ago."

—Johnny, a high school senior

"My best friend, Anna, is one of the most popular girls in school. Anytime we go to the mall or to a party or anywhere, people always want to be with her. She's really pretty and is a lot of fun. She's got great clothes because she's an only child and her parents sort of spoil her. I never have extra money because I have five brothers and sisters. And I'm pretty quiet, and sometimes I just like to read or go to a movie instead of being with a lot of people. I have another friend, Heidi, who is more like me. Lately we've started doing more stuff together. I just feel more comfortable around her. I can be myself. I don't have to try to be somebody else."

—Teena, a high school sophomore

Journal

Reread what you wrote in the "Your Turn" exercise for today, when you identified The Star. Now think about somebody who is more like you, but who has at least a little success doing the same thing that you want to be able to do. Write about that person. How is the person like you? What skills does the person have? How could you use what this person has done to help you achieve what you want to do?

_____

_____

_____

_____

_____

_____

_____

_____

_____

_____

_____

_____

_____

_____

_____

DAY 22   Step 1: Mapping Your Shyness Success

What You Need to Know

For the next six days, we are going to look at ways that you can devise a plan to deal with your shyness. You now understand some of the dynamics of shyness and have looked at some ways to help yourself feel more comfortable. Now it is time to make a plan that will fit you and allow you to proceed at your own pace.

Expanding Your Comfort Zone

The first step in the plan is to expand your comfort zone. Look back at Day 6, where you wrote down physical, social, and personal comfort zones. Now select a personal comfort zone (activity) you would like to expand. It's important to expand gradually, so here are some suggestions:

1. Take what you already feel comfortable doing and see if you can find a way to do a little more of it. That way you will be building on what you already do well.

2. Now take what you do, and do it in a new place or with new people.

3. If it helps, take a person along with you who will help comfort you as you expand to a new place or to new people. (This should remind you of what it was like when you took your favorite teddy bear on your first sleepover when you were six.)

4. Be realistic. It's all right to feel a little uncomfortable when you try something new; just try to stay with it long enough until you begin to feel a little more comfortable. If you start to get really anxious, leave and try again another time.

96

Your Turn

Identify the comfort zone activity you would like to expand.

_____

_____

Describe a way you could do *more* of this activity in the same place and with the same people.

_____

_____

Describe a new place where you would like to do this activity.

_____

_____

Describe a different person you'd like to do this activity with.

_____

_____

Identify a "comfort person" you could take with you when you try the new activity.

_____

_____

Decide what you would consider to be a small success for you as you try the new activity. Keep in mind that you should not expect everything to feel great; it's OK to feel just a little bit more comfortable.

_____

_____

Voices

"I always sit with Sara at lunch. If she's absent, I usually don't even eat lunch. I just go to the library. In a month Sara is going on a Spanish Club trip and will be gone for a week. I don't want to go without lunch for a week. There are a couple of girls we both know a little who also eat together. I'm going to ask Sara whether—before she goes on her trip—she'll go with me to sit with those other girls. That way I'll know somebody else to eat with."

—Mei, a 13-year-old

"I want to ask Jacey to go to the school dance with me. We talk to each other in class and she seems friendly. She even called me a couple of times to talk about homework. The dance is still a few weeks away. I decided to ask her to get pizza with me after school first. That way I can get to know her a little better. Then I can decide about the dance."

—Rob, a high school junior

Journal

Now that you've outlined a plan you can use to expand your comfort zone, write about the way you see that plan developing. Mention when and where you want to try it out. Give yourself a definite date and write that down here as well. Telling someone else (someone safe; someone you trust) what you plan will also help. Can you think of the person you might tell?

_____

_____

_____

_____

_____

_____

_____

_____

_____

_____

_____

_____

_____

_____

_____

DAY 23 Step 2: Surveying the Scene

What You Need to Know

Now that you've secured a plan for expanding your comfort zone and trying something new, it's time to do some preparation: Did you know that when a band is on a road trip, they make sure that somebody has checked out each of the places where they are going to perform so the sound system, the lighting, and the crowd control strategy will all be ready when they get there?

Like the band, you need this kind of preparation as well, considering how you are getting ready to expand your comfort zone to a new place with new people. It should be clear that it is an excellent idea for you to visit your next stop ahead of time. In addition, it is advisable to visit it when nobody is around so you can check the scene without interruption.

Sample Scenario for Surveying the Scene

Felix is working on a group project in his junior history class. The group has been meeting at the city library on Saturday afternoons to work. There is a girl in the group whom Felix likes and would like to date. He usually walks her to the bus stop after leaving the library and waits with her until her bus comes. He asked her to get something to eat with him before she goes home, and she has agreed to do that next week.

But Felix is nervous about the date. So he goes to the pizza place that is near the bus stop. He checks out the prices and the ordering system. He sees that there are tables and booths and realizes he would feel more comfortable in a booth. The waitress tells him that he shouldn't have any problem finding a booth at the time next Saturday that he plans to show up with his friend planning to come. Felix, who was nervous a while ago, now feels relieved because he is a lot more prepared for his date.

Your Turn

Think about the activity that you want to expand to a new place. Then answer the following questions:

Name of activity: _____

Proposed new place: _____

How can you check out the scene ahead of time?

_____

_____

What is it important for you to find out so that you will feel more comfortable?

_____

_____

How can you make sure that you gather the information that you need?

_____

_____

Who could give you some more information about the new place?

_____

_____

Voices

"I really wanted to go to this after-school dance on Fridays. Some of my friends go, so I finally decided to go. But the first time, I wanted just to help out. They let me in a back door, and I helped move the chairs against the walls and set up the tables where they put the cookies. When the doors opened, I was still working, so I didn't feel all scared. I stayed behind the table to hand out drinks. Sometimes I said something. Sometimes I didn't. I didn't dance, but that was OK. I think I'll help out one more time. Then maybe I'll feel OK just to go to the dance."

—Barb, a seventh grader

"We have to do these community service hours at my high school. But I kept putting it off. It means working with a lot of people you don't know. My friend Joe volunteers at a food bank. He let me come with him one Saturday. He introduced me around and showed me different jobs. It really helped to see what you do. I helped the people sorting food for a while. I decided that was OK. You can talk or not talk. So I put my name down to come back. Joe said he'd go the same time I did until I felt comfortable."

—Hakeem, a high school senior

Journal

Write about a time that you arrived at an event early and were able to check out the scene and gradually get comfortable. What was good about that experience? What did you learn about yourself?

_____

_____

_____

_____

_____

_____

_____

_____

_____

_____

_____

_____

_____

_____

_____

DAY 24   Step 3: Practicing What You Do and Say

What You Need to Know

You know that bands practice, basketball players practice, singers practice. Did you know that people also practice what they are going to say? It's true, and not just for speeches.

Why It's Good to Be Prepared to Talk

> *Tricia has decided that she wants to expand her comfort zone in being around boys. She is OK in class because there is something to talk about. Any other time she feels shy. But she likes to play chess, and there are a lot of guys in the chess club. Tricia plays chess with her dad and with her sister and with another girlfriend, but she has never been to the chess club.*
>
> *So she visits the chess club with her girlfriend, who is a member. She watches what happens (checking out the scene) and asks her friend a few questions. Nobody else talks to her, but at least she feels more comfortable.*
>
> *The next week she goes to the chess club with her friend, but her friend has a match to play right away. Tricia is sitting on the sidelines, watching her friend, and a boy sits down next to her. She recognizes him as one of the really good players she watched last week. She totally freezes. She can't think of anything to say. After a minute, she gets up and leaves.*

What Happened?

Tricia needed to practice *precisely* what would happen and what she would say. Sometimes the very first thing you say to someone is the hardest. That's why it is best to be prepared. Tricia learned that she needs to write down several things she could possibly say and then practice saying those comments aloud. It would also be a good idea if she could ask her friend to practice with her. That way there would be somebody to talk back to her.

Your Turn

Think about the activity you want to try in a new place or with new people. You've checked out the scene and know what to expect. Now imagine that you are actually there.

What are you going to do first? Add as many details as possible. You walk into the room (or gym or hallway). Then what?

_____

_____

_____

Write down three things you can say to the first person you talk to. For example, you might ask, "Is this your first time here?" Another question might be, "What do you like about this place?"

_____

_____

_____

What if nobody talks to you? What are you going to do? (Leaving is not an option in this imaginary world!)

_____

_____

_____

Voices

"Well, I finally got up enough courage to sit by somebody else on the bus, instead of sitting by myself, like I always do. I picked someone else who always sits alone. And it's someone I have a class with, so I know him a little bit. I asked if I could sit down. He said, 'Sure.' And that's the last word either of us ever said. Oh, yeah. I said, 'Bye,' when I got off the bus. Does that count?"

—Maryann, a seventh grader

"I like to run after school. It keeps me in shape for baseball season. Most of the time I run by myself on a mile loop that starts at the school and loops through some parking lots and around some buildings and back to where I started. During the baseball season, the team runs together, but now a lot of the guys are playing other sports. I see a guy out running my loop sometimes, but I don't know him. One day I decided to wait for him. When he got to me, I asked if I could run along. He nodded, so we started off. I guess I thought we'd talk about stuff while we ran, like I do with my baseball friends. But it just didn't happen. I'm back to running by myself."

—Aaron, a high school sophomore

Journal

Write about a time you practiced something you were going to do, and it helped you feel more comfortable.

_____

_____

_____

_____

_____

_____

_____

_____

_____

_____

_____

_____

_____

_____

_____

_____

_____

DAY 25 Step 4: Go S-L-O-W

What You Need to Know

We've already discussed how shy individuals take longer than others to adjust to and feel comfortable with a new activity. (If you need a reminder, see Day 5.) The way to deal with this problem is to give yourself more time to warm up in your new situation. What follows are a few tips that may help you while you are giving yourself time to warm up and prepare yourself.

1. Arrive early wherever you have to go so you have time to feel comfortable before a lot of people start showing up.

2. If at all possible, volunteer to help with something (setting up chairs, passing out flyers, putting out food, setting up the chessboards).

3. Remember what you've practiced. Wait for a good time to start your new activity or do something with a new person. (Give yourself plenty of time. There is no hurry.)

4. Look for other individuals who seem to be by themselves. If you've practiced what you are going to say, it can help you feel more comfortable to be with someone else who also is a little hesitant or uncertain.

5. Go slow. Did we say that already? No? Well, keep in mind that it is not only OK to go slow; it's the preferred way.

Your Turn

Again, think about the new activity that you want to try. Let's say you have surveyed the scene and have practiced what you are going to say and do. Before you know it, you are there, in your new situation. Write down three things you can do just to spend some time getting comfortable when you begin the activity. You need to be ready with 15–20 minutes' worth of activities:

1. _____

_____

_____

_____

2. _____

_____

_____

_____

3. _____

_____

_____

_____

What else can you do to make yourself *go slow?*

_____

_____

Voices

"I practiced in front of a mirror so I would have some things to say when I first got to the party. I even tried to make sure I wouldn't frown too much. But when I got there, I almost left. It just felt so scary. But I walked around the edges of the room. I even went into the kitchen and offered to help. They let me take some ice and stuff out to the party. Then I stood by my friend, Pete. He's a good talker. You don't have to say much when Pete's around. In a little while I felt a little more relaxed. It was better after that."

—Jack, a 14-year-old

"We have class discussions in history and get points for talking about the topic for the day. But I hate to talk in class. I just get so scared. My teacher told me I wasn't going to get a good grade unless I could talk in class. But he suggested a way I could deal with how scared I was. Each day he puts a question on the board for homework, and then he starts out class with that question the next day. He asked me to go home and work on the question. He said I should write down my answer. Then he wanted me to practice it in front of the mirror. He told me he would call on me the next day. I went home and did what he said. At first it felt funny to practice in front of a mirror. But I kept doing it until I thought my answer sounded OK. The next day I made sure that I got to class early. I walked around for a minute to calm down, and then I practiced my answer in my head. When the teacher asked the question at the start of class, I raised my hand. He called on me, and I gave the answer I practiced. He said, 'Good point,' and then he called on another person. I felt terrific! Now I'm going to practice answering questions in front of a mirror every day."

—Luisa, a 16-year-old

Journal

Think of a time in the past when you felt really shy during an activity, but you went slow and gave yourself time to feel more comfortable. Now write about it, answering these questions: What did you do to make yourself go slow? How did you feel about what happened when you let yourself take your time?

_____

_____

_____

_____

_____

_____

_____

_____

_____

_____

_____

_____

_____

_____

_____

_____

DAY 26 Step 5: Talking on the Fly

What You Need to Know

Shy individuals often feel uncomfortable talking outside of their comfort zones. Of course, it helps to practice exactly what you are going to say and do in the first few minutes of a new situation. But what about after that? What do you say then?

One way to let other people know you are interested in talking is through "quick talk." Quick talk involves merely saying something nice. That's right: nice. You do it by commenting on something that's going on that everyone would agree with. The best thing about quick talk is that you can practice it anywhere. You don't have to wait for a time when you are trying to expand your comfort zone. Here's an example of how it works:

Jamie walks down the hallway near the lockers. He has decided to try five quick-talk comments this morning. What topics for quick talk are available to him? The following are examples that anyone can use:

+ Weather (a bit lame, perhaps, but always a safe topic): "It's snowing outside."

+ Time of day (first thing in the morning): "Hey, looks like we're all a bit sleepy."

+ Bulletin board item (news of importance to everyone): "Look. It's time to sign up for the SAT."

+ Entertainment for the evening (kids are excited): "Gee, I can't wait for the basketball game tonight."

+ Any shared gripe (common concern): "Wow! Mr. Smith really laid on the English homework yesterday, didn't he?"

You see? Jamie (and other shy teens) have a lot to work with in the way of material for conversation. Nothing is earthshaking; it doesn't have to be. By making a quick comment, Jamie is succeeding in showing people that he's a nice guy, a friendly person who is willing to talk. Jamie walks up to the group standing near his locker and lets fly with one of his quick-talk comments: "Man, can you believe that snow? My feet are soaked."

Everybody grumbles about the homework for a minute, which opens the door for another quick-talk remark by Jamie: As he's taking stuff out of his locker, he says, "Can you believe Mrs. Hoffman gave us all that homework? Doesn't she realize our brains are still on break?"

See? Nothing special. Just a few quick comments. Jamie can choose to stay and talk some more or move on. But he is in the mix. He's not on the sidelines watching everybody else.

Your Turn

Practice your quick talk on paper. Pretend that today you are walking into a social activity with people where you are not totally comfortable. Write down one thing you could say about each of the following:

The weather

_____

_____

The time of day

_____

_____

Something you saw on TV (the hot new show everyone is watching)

_____

_____

Something you heard on the radio (a popular new song)

_____

_____

A shared gripe by your peers

_____

_____

Something exciting that is going to happen (a new movie, a holiday)

_____

_____

Voices

"I usually don't have much to say unless somebody asks me a question. But when I work in the library, I always try to say something to people when I check out their books. I might talk about one of the books they are checking out. Or maybe I notice something they are wearing. Or sometimes I say something about stuff happening at school. It's not too hard. The student is on the way out, so it doesn't last long. But last week somebody told me how nice it was to have such a friendly person working the desk. Somebody called me friendly! Wow!"

—Dorinda, a 15-year-old

"I've gotten better about talking at parties. I finally figured out that it doesn't much matter what you talk about, just so you talk. And sometimes it's better to ask a question. That way it gets somebody else to talk. I usually start with something simple: "What's the best thing you've ever had to eat at a party?" (Or sometimes I ask, "What's the strangest thing you've had to eat?" That always gets some good answers.) I think of questions ahead of time, and that helps. Like if it's a theme party, I can ask a question that has to do with the theme."

—Will, a college freshman

Journal

Think about a time you attended a social activity and felt a little uncomfortable, but someone talked to you and it helped. What did you talk about? How did the conversation get started?

_____

_____

_____

_____

_____

_____

_____

_____

_____

_____

_____

_____

_____

_____

DAY 27   Step 6: Dealing with Rejection

What You Need to Know

What if you do everything suggested in steps 1–5, but you bomb? For example:

+ Somebody walks away from you at a party.
+ Nobody asks you to dance.
+ People talk around you, not to you.
+ You can't find people who will let you sit with them at lunch.

Sure, it's possible for one or more of these incidents to occur. Even if you prepare well, it can happen: It's not likely, but it's still possible. In addition, as a shy teen, you know it's possible. All of this makes it hard for you to step outside your comfort zone.
  So, if it happens to you, how can you deal with rejection?

+ First, realize that rejection hardly ever happens, especially if you prepare well in advance using steps 1–5.
+ Next, look at what happened: Can you learn something about why you were rejected? If you can use this incident as feedback, then it can help you next time. Maybe you chose an unfriendly person to talk to. Or maybe you tried to sit with the biggest snobs in school. Or maybe you asked too many questions and that put people on guard.
+ Finally, make a plan to try again. Rejection happens to everybody. (Yes, believe it or not, *everybody!*) So use the feedback, go through the steps once again, and expect to succeed this time around.

Your Turn

Think about a time you tried a new social activity. Maybe you even used some of the suggestions provided in this book to deal with your shyness, but still you felt rejected. Answer each of the following questions:

What was the activity?

_____

_____

How did you prepare to deal with your shyness?

_____

_____

What happened to make you feel rejected?

_____

_____

Looking back, what can you learn from this experience?

_____

_____

What would you do differently next time?

_____

_____

Voices

"OK, so I tried something new. My friends have been bugging me to join the Pep Club. They know I like sports. I go to all the games. But there are a lot of popular people in the Pep Club. Popular people don't like me. And I was right. I went to the first meeting, but nobody talked to me. I sat there and people ignored me. My friend said she tried to help me get in the conversation. But I guess I was too scared to talk. I don't know if I have the guts to try again."

—Winnie, a high school sophomore

"I like playing video games at the mall. I usually play by myself, and on some games I'm pretty good. But there's a group of guys who play together on Saturday. One of them invited me to come. I went one week and just watched to figure out what's what. I thought it was pretty safe. So I went the next week and took a turn playing. I could tell that one guy really didn't want me there. But the rest seemed OK with me. I decided it was his problem. I'm going back next week."

—Vince, a 14-year-old

Journal

Everybody does get rejected, but shy individuals seem to be more hurt by rejection. What makes rejection hard for you? How do you feel about yourself when you are rejected? What have you learned about dealing with shyness that will also help you deal with your feelings about being rejected?

_____

_____

_____

_____

_____

_____

_____

_____

_____

_____

_____

_____

_____

_____

DAY 28 You're in Charge!

What You Need to Know

If you've been following the five steps, you've gone outside your comfort zone and tried something new. That's great! Doing something new is never easy, and that's especially true if you're a shy teen. So give yourself a pat on the back, a high five, a gold star, whatever makes you feel good. In no way is this a minor accomplishment of yours.

So what's next? You probably want to keep trying to do some small things to expand your comfort zone. But it's very important for *you* to decide what you're going to do and when. Don't let anyone else try to talk you into something you're not ready to do.

Sometimes teens (and adults) who aren't shy don't understand why you should feel uncomfortable if they don't. Now that you've been to one party, they figure, you should be ready to go anywhere. Here's a good place to take a time-out.

This is your life, and you're the one who knows when you feel uncomfortable. It's OK to take small steps. In fact, that's the very best way to do things. As long as you are taking steps to deal with your shyness, it doesn't matter how slow you go. You are the one who decides what it takes for you to feel comfortable. Maybe there are certain times when it's not worth the effort (for example, you hate to dance, so why go?). Save your energy for things you care about—not what others think you should care about.

It's true that refusing to listen to other people tell you what you "should" do may be one of the hardest things about dealing with your shyness. Yet you are the expert on you. You are the *only* one who knows what you need to do to be successfully shy.

When somebody tries to push you, you don't need to give a reason why you don't want to do something. It's enough for you to say, "I don't want to"—over and over again.

Example:

Go-getter George: Hey, you should go to the party. You'll have a great time.

Shy Steve: Thanks, but that's not a party where I'd feel comfortable.

Go-getter George: But it's a lot of fun. I'll bet if you try, you'll like it.

Shy Steve: No, thanks.

Go-getter George: Everybody will be there. Don't be a jerk.

Shy Steve: "You go. Tell me about it. See you later."

As Shy Steve showed, it's important not to get in an argument with someone who thinks he's looking out for your best interests. After all, Go-getter George simply wanted Steve to go to the party with him, and he had trouble understanding why Steve couldn't see the situation the way he did. To his credit, Steve held his ground. He remembered what he had learned about himself and his shyness: He—and nobody else—is the person who's in charge of what he does.

Your Turn

Sometimes there are people who can be helpful to you as you try out your new skills in an attempt to become successfully shy. Then there are those people who always think you should be doing more to deal with your shyness. Read the following comments and questions and write down your thoughts:

Name a good friend of yours who is supportive of you when you begin to step outside your comfort zone. What does this friend do to help?

_____

_____

Name a friend who is always trying to push you to do more than you are ready to do. How does this friend push too hard?

_____

_____

Write down two things you can say to the friend who pushes too hard that will make it clear that you are in charge of your shyness.

_____

_____

Name an adult who is supportive of you when you begin to step outside your comfort zone. What does this adult do to help?

_____

_____

Name an adult who is always trying to push you to do more than you are ready to do. How does this adult push too hard?

_____

_____

Write down two things you can say to this adult that will show that you are in charge of your shyness.

_____

_____

Voices

"Marianne kept bugging me to go out for cheerleader. She cheers and she's a good friend, but that's really not my thing. But she kept at me, so finally I gave in. I practiced with her, but I still did a miserable job at tryouts. I didn't even make the first cut. I know everybody is laughing at me. I wish I could have figured out a way to say no to her."

—Carolyn, a high school freshman

"My mom told me she was always pretty shy when she was in middle school. She says she's still shy sometimes, but that it was worse back then. She understands what it's like. One time some new friends asked me to meet them at the mall, but I was scared. My mom took me to the mall to meet the group, and she did her own shopping. I asked her to call me in an hour on my cell phone. If I wasn't comfortable, I was going to pretend she needed me to come home. But things were OK, so I stayed. It was great to know she was a backup."

—Riana, a sixth grader

"I felt really good when I went to my first school dance. It was a big step for me. I stayed a whole hour without feeling uncomfortable. Now my friend Joey wants me to go to a dance at another school. But I told him no. I'm not ready for that. I told him my next goal was to stay the whole time for a dance at our school without feeling uncomfortable."

—Philippe, a high school junior

Journal

Now that you have successfully stepped outside your comfort zone once, write about the next goals that you want to set for yourself. Attach a "trial date" to some of these goals, but remember to take small steps that fit you. Listen to your voice, not the voices of others.

_____

_____

_____

_____

_____

_____

_____

_____

_____

_____

_____

_____

_____

_____

DAY 29 Helping Yourself by Helping Others

What You Need to Know

Sometimes it's hard to practice your new skills with the people you see every day. Maybe they expect you to be shy. Or maybe you've already had a bad experience with some of them, which makes trying something new harder. Do you wish you could just start over somewhere else? Maybe you can.

Why not try being a volunteer? Community agencies are always on the lookout for volunteers, and they are usually ready to welcome any help. The Voluntary Action Center is listed in the phone book in most communities and can give you information on places that can accept teenagers. (Some places have minimum age limits for some volunteers.) If you don't have a Voluntary Action Center in your community, call the United Way or check with a local church. Somebody always needs help.

How Volunteering Can Help Reduce Your Shyness

1. Volunteers have specific jobs, so there is some structure to what you do.
2. The people you work with will be happy to have your help and will go out of their way to make you feel comfortable.
3. Not a lot is expected of volunteers, especially at the beginning. There isn't much pressure placed on you.
4. Volunteering will give you new social contacts.
5. Volunteering will give you a new place to try out your social skills.

When deciding on a place to volunteer, remember your comfort zones. It's good, for example, to start with something that you feel comfortable doing. Maybe you know others who volunteer, and you can go with them. Or maybe your own church needs help. Or maybe there is a volunteer job that uses a skill that you have. For instance, if you don't like animals, don't volunteer at the animal shelter. Instead, use your good computer skills to teach kids and senior citizens at the community center how to search the Internet for information.

Your Turn

List five jobs you think you might like to do as a volunteer:

1. _____

2. _____

3. _____

4. _____

5. _____

Note the age group you think you would feel most comfortable working with: _____

Contact someone in your community who coordinates volunteer work. Tell the person the age group you want to work with and mention some of your own skills. After you receive information from the coordinator, list a few of the jobs you would be interested in volunteering to do:

1. _____

2. _____

3. _____

4. _____

5. _____

Voices

"I started helping out at a nursing home near my school last month. I try to go twice a week after school, and sometimes I go on Saturday. I read to some people and write letters for others whose hands aren't steady enough to write. And sometimes I wheel people out onto the patio and we just enjoy the sun together. They are always so happy to see me, it makes me feel great. A lot of the staff know my name now, and they don't treat me like a kid. They treat me more like an adult, and I like that."

—Jana, a 15-year-old

"My school makes us do a hundred hours of community service before we graduate. I was really dreading it because I don't like to be around strangers. I talked to our volunteer coordinator, and I even visited a couple of places before deciding. Now I help plant flowers and trim shrubs at the public buildings in town. I've always liked growing stuff, and my neighbor is the crew boss. I don't have to talk a lot, and I look forward to going."

—Martin, a high school senior

Journal

Now that you've investigated some volunteer possibilities, which ones appeal to you the most? Why do these catch your interest? How will they help you step outside your comfort zone at a pace that is right for you?

_____

_____

_____

_____

_____

_____

_____

_____

_____

_____

_____

_____

_____

DAY 30   Somebody Else Is Shyer than You

What You Need to Know

As you continue to learn to deal with your own shyness, you will become more aware of people around you who are also shy. The major difference, though, is that you will also notice that—unlike you—most of these individuals (both teens and adults) are not successfully shy. Because of your own experiences with shyness, you will be able to understand how they feel. And because you understand what they are going through, you will be able to help them. Exactly how can you help them? Here are some simple ideas:

✦ When you see people who are by themselves and seem uncomfortable, go over and talk to them. Introduce yourself and make a few quick-talk comments.

> If things go well with one person, you can continue talking. If possible, introduce your new shy friend to somebody else. Draw your new friend into the conversation.

> If you've already discovered something that the new shy person likes to do, bring up that topic so you can begin a discussion that will help him or her forget about being shy.

✦ Or let's say you are with a group of people who are engaged in conversation. In time, you become aware that one person isn't saying anything and seems to be on the fringes of the group:

> Ask that person a question or ask his or her opinion on a topic.

> In general, help the person become a part of the conversation.

As you continue to help shy people, you will find not only that they are benefiting from your assistance, but that you yourself are benefiting from helping them. You'll be thinking so much about helping shy people feel comfortable, you will soon notice something new: Although you're still shy, you're no longer the shy person you were before you began reading this book—back when you were concerned and mystified about your shyness and didn't realize there was a way to become *successfully* shy.

Your Turn

Think of a recent social event you took part in (for example, a school-wide lunch, a club meeting, a party) where you used to be extremely shy but are now feeling much more comfortable because you've started using some of the successfully shy skills you've read about and written about. Now close your eyes and scan the room in your mind.

Who else at this event is also shy? How can you tell?

_____

_____

_____

List several things you could have done to help this person feel more comfortable:

a. _____

_____

_____

b. _____

_____

_____

c. _____

_____

_____

Voices

"Jojo and I used to always eat lunch by ourselves. But I've been practicing my new skills and got up the nerve to ask some other guys I know to sit with us. That's been going really well. But last week I noticed the new kid was eating alone. I asked him if he wanted to sit with us. He didn't have much to say until I asked him about the motorcycle patch on his jacket. He's a neat guy!"

—Turk, a seventh grader

"It felt so good to finally be comfortable at the Spanish Club meetings. I'm not the best Spanish student, but I like practicing my conversations. We're not supposed to use any English during the meetings, and that makes me a little nervous. I noticed this girl from my class who wasn't saying much while we were eating. I asked her something, and I tried to speak slowly so she would understand me. She answered back, even though she stumbled over some of the words. I smiled to show her it was OK. We said some more things to each other and laughed at our mistakes. Next meeting I am going to try to sit by her."

—Gretchen, a ninth grader

Journal

Feeling comfortable enough to help other shy people is a big step on your journey toward being successfully shy. If you have been able to do this, write about what has happened and how you have begun to feel differently about yourself.

_____

_____

_____

_____

_____

_____

_____

_____

_____

_____

_____

_____

_____

_____

EPILOGUE Living the Successfully Shy Life

What You Need to Know

During the past 30 days, you have learned a lot of new skills for living a successfully shy life. Does this mean you will now be a different person? No. You are still you. You are still shy, but now when shyness keeps you from doing something that you want to do, you have some tools to use to aid you in any number of situations.

So where do you go from here? It is possible that every day you will be faced with some discomfort because you are shy. This will not change in a month or six months. It's just like learning any new skill. It takes a lot of practice. Change is gradual. Sorry—there is no magic wand.

But if you have tried any of the activities in this book, you have started on the path to dealing with your shyness. That is terrific! Now take another step. It doesn't matter how small that step is. Just keep taking those small steps, and gradually you will feel more comfortable.

✳ ✽ ✳

As an aid, try the following: In six months, go back and read some of your answers to the "Your Turn" exercises. If you wrote out some of the "Journal" entries, read those, too. It is very likely that you will not be dealing with the same things you wrote about this month. You will have moved on to other things. You may not even notice it, but that is progress!

And that's what living the successfully shy life is all about: It's about making progress little by little so that being shy doesn't stop you from doing what you want to do. Being successfully shy is yours for the taking. Go for it!

Your Turn

Look back at the goals that you set on Day 9. You've probably already worked on some of them. You also might have added some other goals or identified some other situations that will enable you to work on those goals. Now answer the following questions:

1. What is the No. 1 goal you want to work on in dealing with your shyness?

    _____

    _____

    _____

    _____

2. What is the specific situation related to this goal that you want to work on first?

    _____

    _____

    _____

    _____

3. Which of the skills that you've learned to use to deal with your shyness would help you achieve this goal?

    _____

    _____

    _____

    _____

Make a Plan

Write out a plan of action and estimate how long it might take you to try working on the goals you've set for yourself to make your plan a success (for example, tomorrow, in a week, by next month). Making specific action plans will help you achieve your goal.

Step 1: _____

_____

Try by _____

Step 2: _____

_____

Try by _____

Step 3: _____

_____

Try by _____

Voices

"I write down the things I want to do and tape them to the inside of my closet door. That way I see my plan every day. If I chicken out, I'll write down a new day to try. Sometimes if I am really worried about trying something new, I'll tell my friend Jerry. He won't push me, but he will ask me how things went. That way I won't chicken out."

—Mark, a 15-year-old

"My school counselor helped me figure out some things I could do when I was feeling shy. I like to drop by and see her every few weeks. I always try to have one new thing I can tell her that I've tried. She's always so happy for me. That makes me feel good."

—Roberta, a high school freshman

"I figured I was always going to be shy and miserable. It's still not easy, but I do more things than I used to do. Sometimes I have to practice saying stuff for a week before I can talk to somebody new. But it gets a little easier. That's something."

—Susie, a high school senior

Journal

Think of yourself one year from now. If you keep working on the goals you have set, what do you hope to be doing by then?

_____

_____

_____

_____

_____

_____

_____

_____

_____

_____

_____

_____

_____

_____

_____

_____

_____

_____

Selected Bibliography

If you would like more information about shyness and the topics discussed in *The Shyness Workbook for Teens,* we recommend that you go to the Indiana University Southeast Shyness Research Institute Web site at www.isu.edu/shyness or read any of the following:

Carducci, B. J. (1999b). *The Pocket Guide to making successful small talk: How to talk to anyone anytime anywhere about anything.* New Albany, IN: Pocket Guide Publishing.

Carducci, B. J. (2000a). *Shyness: A bold new approach.* New York: HarperPerennial.

Carducci, B. J. (2000b, February). Shyness: The new solution. *Psychology Today, 33,* 38–40, 42–45, 78.

Carducci, B. J. (2000c). What shy individuals do to cope with their shyness: A content analysis. In W. Ray Crozier (Ed.), *Shyness: Development, consolidation and change* (pp. 171–185). New York: Routledge.

Carducci, B. J. (2001). Are we born shy? The Psychology Place [On line, Archive: Op Ed Forum, February 2001] Available: http://psych-place.com/archives/editorials.

Carducci, B. J. (2003). *The shyness breakthrough: A no-stress plan to help your shy child warm up, open up, and join the fun.* Emmaus, PA: Rodale.

Carducci, B. J. (2005). *The shyness workbook: 30 days to dealing effectively with shyness.* Champaign, IL: Research Press.

Carducci, B. J., & Zimbardo, P. G. (1995, November/December). Are you shy? *Psychology Today, 28,* 34–41, 64, 66, 68, 70, 78, 82.

Zimbardo, P. G. (1990). *Shyness: What it is, what to do about it* (Reissued ed.). Reading, MA: Addison-Wesley.

Zimbardo, P. G., & Radl. S. L. (1979). *The shyness workbook.* New York: A & W Visual Library.

Zimbardo, P. G., & Radl, S. L. (1999). *The shy child: A parent's guide to preventing and overcoming shyness in infancy to adulthood* (2nd ed.). Cambridge, MA: Malor Books.

About the Authors

Bernardo J. Carducci (Ph.D., Kansas State University, 1981) is a full professor of psychology and director of the Shyness Research Institute at Indiana University Southeast, a fellow of the American Psychological Association, and a member of *Who's Who in Frontier Science and Technology.*

In addition to *The Shyness Workbook for Teens,* he has authored the following books: *Shyness: A Bold New Approach* (2000a, HarperPerennial); *The Shyness Breakthrough: A No-Stress Plan to Help Your Shy Child Warm Up, Open Up, and Join the Fun* (2003, Rodale); *The Shyness Workbook: 30 Days to Dealing Effectively with Shyness* (Research Press, 2005); *The Pocket Guide to Making Successful Small Talk: How to Talk to Anyone Anytime Anywhere About Anything* (1999, Pocket Guide Publishing); and *The Psychology of Personality: Viewpoints, Research, and Applications* (1998, Brooks/Cole Publishers).

Dr. Carducci has appeared numerous times on ABC-TV's *Good Morning America* and other national and international media services, such as the BBC. His writing and advice have been featured in a number of diverse magazines and newspapers, including among others, *Psychology Today, U.S. News & World Report, USA Weekend, Vogue, Allure, YM, TWA Ambassador, Glamour, JET, Parenting, Walking, Self, Good Housekeeping, JANE, Essence, Child, Reader's Digest, Parents, Fitness, Redbook, First for Women, The Futurist, Entrepreneur, The Wall Street Journal, The Chicago Tribune, The London Times, The Los Angeles Times,* and *The New York Times.*

* ❊ *

Teesue H. Fields (Ed.D., Rutgers University, 1975) is a full professor of education and coordinator of counselor education at Indiana University Southeast. She is a member of the American Counseling Association and the American School Counseling Association and past president of the Indiana Counseling Association. She is a nationally certified counselor. She worked as a psychologist in private practice, as a school counselor, as a school psychologist, and as a high school teacher before coming to the university to teach. All of her psychology and counseling jobs have involved children and adolescents.

Dr. Fields has published book chapters and journal articles on group counseling, individual counseling techniques, and the role of the school counselor in helping students achieve success in school. She is married and is the mother of two grown sons.